JOHN G. PATON

Missionary to the New Hebrides

An Autobiography Edited
by His Brother . . . . .

VOLUME III.

With a Historical Note and an Account of the
Progress of the Gospel in the New Hebrides

Illustrated

NEW YORK   CHICAGO   TORONTO
Fleming H. Revell Company
Publishers of Evangelical Literature

EDITOR'S PREFACE.

THE Autobiography of my brother, Dr. John G. Paton has now, at my urgent entreaty, been continued by him, and carried on to the present year.

It tells the Story of the Life during the twelve years that have elapsed since Part First and Part Second were completed by the Author, and separately given to the world.

The following words from the *Preface* to an early Edition of the Autobiography are equally applicable to present circumstances:— "The Public hailed it from the first with a welcome so uncommon, and God has in many ways so signally owned and blessed it, that it would be no modesty, but sheer stupidity, on my part, to fail in recognizing that it has been voted a Missionary Classic by the great and free Community of Readers. I have therefore spared no pains in making it as perfect as it is in my power to do, with the help of many minute corrections from friends here and abroad, and also happy suggestions as to matters of detail from the honored Missionary himself."

In the original *Preface* when the book was first published in 1889, I said: "The Manuscript of this Volume, put together in a rough draft amid ceaseless and exacting toils, was placed in my hands and left absolutely to my disposal by my beloved brother, the Missionary. It has been to me a labor of perfect love to re-write and revise the same, pruning here and expanding there, and, preparing the whole for the press. In the incidents of personal experience, constituting the larger part of the book, the reader peruses in an almost unaltered form the graphic and simple narrative as it came from my brother's pen. But, as many sections have been re-cast and largely modified, especially in those Chapters of whose events I was myself an eyewitness, or regarding which I had information at first hand from the parties concerned therein,—and as circumstances make it impossible to submit these in their present shape to my brother before publication,—I must request the Public to lay upon me, and not on him, all responsibility for the final shape in which the Autobiography appears. I publish it because Something tells me there is a blessing in it."

That belief was abundantly justified. The book has had a great circulation, not only in Great Britain, but also in America, and in the Colonies; and it has been translated, in whole or in part, into many Modern Languages.   JAMES PATON.

GLASGOW, *February*, 1898.

3

CONTENTS.

CHAPTER I.

ROUND THE WORLD FOR JESUS.

5

CHAPTER II.

THE HOME-LANDS AND THE ISLANDS.

LIST OF ILLUSTRATIONS.

For the use of all the above illustrations, save the first, our acknowl-
edgments are due to " The Missionary Review of the World."

Historical Note.

BALBOA, governor of Santa Maria, discovered the Southern Ocean in 1513, named it the South Sea, and took possession in the name of the king of Spain. Six years later Magellan sailed through a large portion of it, and called it the Pacific Ocean. In 1569 Mendana discovered and named the Solomon group, and in 1595 the Queen Charlotte group. The New Hebrides were discovered in 1606 by Quiros, who thought he had discovered a great southern continent, and called it the Land of the Holy Spirit. He anchored in port Philip Santo, and tried to establish a city (New Jerusalem) on the bank of the large river Yor, which runs into the bay. But the Spaniards quarrelled with the natives and left it. Quiros sailed to Mexico, but Torres, the senior officer in command, sailed west, discovered and passed through Torres Straits, which bear his name, between Queensland and New Guinea. Boginville discovered that it was not a continent, but a group of islands, that Quiros had discovered, and he named them the Great Cyclades. Bent on discovering new lands, about that period many eminent navigators sailed in the South Sea, but we hear nothing more of the New Hebrides till, in 1767, the famous Captain Cook sailed on his first voyage to observe the transit of Venus at Tahiti. In 1773 Captain Cook returned, and sailed twice through the group, spending forty-six days in exploring and describing every island and the natives with an accuracy scarcely yet surpassed. Believing he had discovered the most westerly group in the South Sea, he gave it its present name, the New Hebrides ; but 200 miles southwest he afterward discovered another large island, and called it New Caledonia. He took possession of it in the name of his sovereign, King George the Third ; but in 1854, when Britain was engaged in the Crimean war, France took possession of it, and turned it into a large convict station at the door of Australia, to which, by escaped convicts, it is a source of danger and pollution.—J. G. P.

The Gospel in the New Hebrides. [1]

BY REV. JOHN G. PATON, D. D.

GEOGRAPHERS have arranged the South Sea islands under three divisions : Polynesia, the many eastern islands between 180 degrees and South America ; Melanesia, the black islands, from the dark-brown color of their inhabitants—they include Fiji and all the islands west, with New Guinea ; Micronesia, all the small islands north of the line from Hawaii on the east to China on the west. The South Sea islands are inhabited by only two races, the Malay Polynesian and the Papuan. The Malays appear to be of Asiatic origin, and are the superior race, with well-developed, powerful persons, yellow in color, and with straight, glossy, black hair. The Papuans are so called from Papua, or New Guinea. They occupy the western islands, and are not generally so tall and handsome in person as the Malays. They are of a dark-brown color, with dark, curly hair of different shades, and appear to be allied to the negro ; but have plump, pleasant features, unlike the negro and the aborigines of Australia. The Malays all speak one language, with dialectic differences, all musical and liquid, like the

[1] *From " The Missionary Review of the World."*

Italian. Every word ends in a vowel. The Papuans speak a different language on almost every island, or dialects differing, so that the natives of one island can-not understand those of another; and on some islands two or even three dialects are spoken on the same island, so different that the inhabitants of the one dis-trict cannot understand those of the other. Nearly the whole, if not the whole, population of the South Sea islands were cannibals, in a state of nudity, when missionary work was begun on them, yet even there, by God's blessing, almost every society and church en-gaged in the work has been used and honored in the conversion of many thousands, and now each is work-ing on an independent portion of New Guinea for the salvation of its natives, and with encouraging success.

The New Hebrides consist of about thirty inhabited islands, with many small ones adjoining. The group lies south-southeast and north-northwest, extending over 400 miles of ocean, between 21 degrees and 15 degrees south latitude, and 171 degrees and 166 de-grees east longitude. The Solomon group, which is the centre of the Church of England's mission, is about 200 miles northwest from the New Hebrides. New Caledonia is about 200 miles southwest, Fiji about 400 miles, Auckland about 1,000, and Sydney, Australia, 1,400 miles distant from our group. In her first charter to New Zealand, Britain included the New Hebrides, but, apparently by some mistake, they were afterward left out. Yet, except to New Zealand and Australia, the group is of little commercial value to

any other country, on account of the great distances
of all others from it.

As the natives have got nearly all the blessings of
Christianity and civilization which they possess from
British missionaries and subjects, they unanimously
plead for British annexation and protection, while,
from their oppressive cruelty to the natives, and suppression of Protestant schools and mission work on
the Loyalty group and on other groups annexed, they
fear and hate the French. There are other cogent
reasons, for the French Senate passed a resolution " to
send 100,000 of France's lowest criminals to the New
Hebrides, as freed men and women, to live as they
could and go where they would, on the one condition
that they do not return to France." Against this
Australasia and Britain protested so decidedly that the
scheme was not carried out ; but the resolution to de-
port them was renewed, and for the present the destination is kept secret. The French have recently been
sending Roman Catholic priests to the New Hebrides,
apparently as political agents. A few months ago the
heathen natives of one of our islands eagerly desired
a Protestant missionary to settle among them, and
give them the teaching of Jesus and His salvation,
and when they were selling our missionaries a site for
the station, two priests gave them much abuse, and
told them of all the fearful calamities which would be-
fall them if they allowed the Protestant missionaries to
land on their island. They also gave the missionaries
much abuse, and at last offered the natives three

Sniders (rifles) and two large, fat hogs for the site, if they would forbid the Protestant missionaries to settle on the island. Though, above everything else, the heathen islanders desire Sniders and such fat pigs, yet they rejected the priests' offer, and sold the station to our missionaries. The highest French officials in these colonies have sent a man-of-war to the spot to investigate this case, and their report proves that it was correctly stated by us.

In 1839 the famous John Williams and Mr. J. Harris, of the London Missionary Society, sailed to try and begin mission work on the New Hebrides, but on landing on Erromanga both were murdered by the savages, who feasted on their bodies. In 1843 Drs. Turner and Nisbet were by the London Missionary Society settled on Tanna, but about six months after, by a passing ship, they had to escape for their lives. After this Samoan and Raratongan native teachers were again and again placed on the group, but they were either murdered by the savages, or died in the damp, unhealthy climate (compared with their own), or in sickness had to be taken home again. So no effective mission work was done on the group till in 1848 Dr. John Geddie and in 1852 Dr. John Inglis were landed on Aneityum, where God spared and used them in bringing 3,500 cannibals on that island to serve our dear Lord Jesus Christ; and until they had translated and carried through the press the whole Bible and other books in their language. For the printing and binding of this Bible the converted na-

WILLIAMS RIVER, ERROMANGA.

The point on the shore where natives stand is that on which John Williams was murdered.

tives paid the noble British and Foreign Bible Society £1,200 sterling ($6,000), earned by them preparing and selling arrowroot.

In 1857 the Rev. G. N. and Mrs. Gordon were placed on Erromanga, where Williams lost his life. By them God brought some fourteen young men and as many young women to renounce heathenism and serve Jesus, but in 1851 the savages one morning tomahawked both to death. Their young converts wept and wailed over their loss, laid them in the grave, and vowed over it that they would conquer Erromanga for Jesus, or die, as their missionaries had died, in the effort. In 1864 the Rev. J. D. Gordon, going to convert, if possible, the murderers of his brother and his wife, was placed on Erromanga, and after much successful work, the heathen there killed him also with the tomahawk in 1872. The Christian party laid his body in the grave, wept and wailed over it, and renewed their vow and wrought and prayed till they have, indeed, conquered the island for Jesus Christ. Now every family there daily sings the praise of His redeeming love, and tries to serve Him devotedly.

In 1858 the Revs. Joseph Copeland, J. W. and Mrs. Matheson, John G. and Mrs. Paton, and in 1859 S. F. and Mrs. Johnston were all placed on Tanna, but soon after Mr. Copeland went to Aneityum. From the first on Tanna, as on other islands, the native priests gave much opposition to the missionaries' teaching. This priesthood is powerful and profess to have and, by sorcery, to exercise all the powers of God. After the

murder of the Gordons, a Tanna "holy" man, prej-
udiced by white traders, clubbed an Aneityum chief, a
native teacher, and he died soon after, rejoicing in Jesus
Christ.   Also from the effects of a savage attack upon
my life and his, Mr. Johnston never rallied, but died
soon after, having been only about four months on the
island.   In 1862, after much suffering, bereavement,
and many attempts upon our lives, and the loss of all
earthly property, except our pocket Bibles, Mr. and
Mrs. Matheson, the teachers, and I escaped by a passing ship.   After reaching Aneityum Mrs. Matheson
died in March and Mr. Matheson in June of that year.
I left for Australia to get, if possible, more missionaries
and a mission ship for our mission.   There the Lord,
by His people, gave me £5,000.   The new *Dayspring*
was bought with £3,000 of it, and the remaining
£2,000 sent and supported more missionaries.   Since
that time island after island has been occupied, and the
Lord has prospered our work, till we have now the
large staff of 26 earnest, educated missionaries, 5 of
them medical men and 5 lay helpers, besides about
300 native teachers, all educated by our own missionaries for their work.   In the mission we have a
teachers' training institution, with 46 students, under
the care of Dr. Annand and his lay teachers, and we
have a hospital under the care of Dr. Lamb and his lay
helpers.   By our missionaries the whole Bible has been
translated into one language, and the New Testament
into several.   The portions of Scripture so translated,
have been printed, and are now read by the natives in

over twenty languages of the group. This is a great work, which makes our mission laborious and expensive compared with others having only one language to conquer. Our islanders had no written language when we began the Lord's work among them. A number of the translations have been printed by the British and Foreign Bible Society, but our natives try to pay it for all it does for them.

As results of the work, our dear Lord Jesus has given our missionaries about 16,000 converts, and the blessed work is extending among some 40,000 or 50,000 remaining cannibals on the group. In our synod year of 1895–96, 1,120 savages renounced idolatry and embraced the worship and service of Christ. One missionary baptized 200 out of his communicants' class of 400, after a long and careful preparatory Scripture training. We never baptize and teach afterward, but educate and wait till they give real evidence of consecration to Jesus Christ, and then, at their desire, baptize, and continue teaching them to observe in their life and conduct all things Jesus has commanded. Hence, we have only about 2,500 communicants, though 10,000 attend our day and Sabbath-schools. All of our converts attend church regularly. In 1896 they contributed about £900, and last year over £1,300 by money and arrowroot, and a number of the islands now support their own native teachers. Yet they have no money but what they get by selling pigs, fowls, cocoanuts, and copra to passing ships. God has given four of our present missionaries each

2

from 1,700 to 2,000 converts; and at all our more recently occupied stations the work is very encouraging, and enjoys the divine blessing. Our chief concern at present is how we are to get money to keep our large staff going on, but we trust in Jesus to provide all as it is needed.

Never since Jesus Christ gave the great commission, have so many of His servants been proclaiming the blessed Gospel, and never before in heathen lands has it shown more vitality and power in its grand results. Yet what large portions of the world are yet in heathen darkness! Oh, for a new Pentecostal baptism of the Holy Spirit to all branches of the Church, to lead her to try to "preach the Gospel to every creature," and by the Gospel conquer the world for Jesus Christ. A small book, showing the extension and glorious fruits of Christian Protestant missions during the last half century would do much to silence the infidel and the enemies of Protestant missions to the heathen, enlighten the indifferent, and draw forth the united praise and prayers, and increased money support, and personal, zealous coöperation of Christians in all lands, so to conquer the world for Jesus Christ by His own appointed means. It would show that the Gospel is not only the power of God unto salvation to every one who believes, high and low, of every color and of every country, but that, wherever found, it is the only real and lasting civilizer of man. Had Britain felt her responsibility, and improved her privileges by spending a twentieth part of what her present wars will cost her

to subdue her rebellious subjects, in giving them the
Gospel teaching of Jesus while under her care, it
might have prevented those wars, and saved her the
loss of life and treasure and carnage in subduing her
heathen revolted subjects, and the feelings of revenge
that remain and foster in the hearts of the surviving
relatives and tribes of the subdued. Armies may conquer and sweep the oppressed into eternity, but Christ's
teaching enlightens the. mind, influences the heart by
creating it anew, and leads all so_ brought under its.
power to feel their responsibility to our God, the
Supreme Judge of all. Thus it lifts them above
heathen superstitions, prejudices, cruelties, and dis-
content, filling the heart with gratitude to God for
His love and mercy in Jesus Christ, and so leading
them to love their benefactors, and to do to others as
they would have others do to them. Though our
New Hebridean savage cannibals, as they all were
when our work began among them, have lost many
thousands of lives, and suffered much oppressive
cruelty by the sandalwood traders and by the shocking
Kanaka labor traffic which followed, yet because of
British missionaries so many of them have been
brought to serve Jesus, that now the remaining population all plead for British annexation and protection.
And lately, on a recently occupied island, where all
under the missionaries' charge were painted savages,
after several acts of kindness by the missionary, the
war chief was led to hear the teaching of Jesus, and to
believe in, and serve Him. He was the first man

among some 3,000 or 4,000 to appear at the church and to wear clothing in public. For some reason his savage warriors wanted him to go to war, but he refused. His enemies sent a man to conceal himself by the path and shoot dead one of the chief's men, being one of their usual challenges to war, and many now urged him to fight in revenge, but he said, " I will not fight and shed blood, but leave all revenge to my Jesus now," and he preached the Gospel of peace and love to them, and prayed for them all. His life was threatened, but he also left that to Jesus. He now teaches a school among his savages, and, following his example, many have begun to wear clothing and attend school and church. The chief and twelve others are now candidates in a class for baptism and church-membership, and a real work of grace seems to have begun all around among the savages. Surely the Divine blessing on the same teaching would produce like blessed results among the heathen subjects of all nations, and make them happy, industrious, loyal, loving subjects—a thing which cannot be done by conquering armies.

I.

ROUND THE WORLD FOR JESUS.

A. D. 1886—1893. ÆT. 62—69.

INTRODUCTORY NOTE.

THE Story of my Life, so unexpectedly owned and blessed of God to multitudes in every Land, closed, when first published in 1889, with what I then regarded and described as my " Last " Visit to Britain, 1884–1885. It did not for one moment enter my mind, at that time, that world-wide travels were still before me, in the interests of our beloved Mission; or that I should ever again be called upon to lift my pen, in the further telling of my own Biography. So much so, that I then wrote something in the " farewell " to the reader, hinting not dimly that the *last* Chapter of all, yet to be added, would fall to be described by another hand than mine!

More than ten years have, however, since elapsed, and " by the good hand of my God upon me for good," I am still hale and vigorous, rejoicing to serve my Redeemer by serving those whom He died to save and lives to bring to Glory. Wherefore, at the earnest and repeated entreaty of my dear brother, James, but for whom this book never could or would have been given to the world at all, I resume my pen to add a brief sketch of the Autumn of my life, that he may set it in order, and bring this *Autobiography* up to date. In many respects, I can unfeignedly say that I would rather bury all in oblivion, or keep it under the eye of my Saviour alone. But I dare not shrink from the door of Great Opportunity thus opened before me; and this, also, I humbly lay on the Altar to the glory of Jesus my Lord.

CHAPTER I.

ROUND THE WORLD FOR JESUS.

A. D. 1886—1893. ÆT. 62—69.

From 1886 to 1892.—Tour Round the World.—Fire-Arms and
Intoxicants.—International Prohibition Proposed.—Depu-
ties to America.—Samoan Converts.—America and Hawaii.
—San Francisco.—Salt Lake City.—Chicago.—Niagara.
—Pan-Presbyterian Council at Toronto.—The Ruthven Im-
posture.—Sabbath Observance.—Rochester.—New York.
—Public Petitions.—Washington.—The Presbyterian As-
sembly.—President Cleveland.—France's Withdrawal.—
Dr. Joseph Cook.—Dr. Blank.—Second Probation.—
Chicago Exhibition.—Canadian Presbyterian Church.—
Two months' Rush of Meetings.—Incidents of Travel.—
Impressions of Canada and the States.

FROM 1886 till 1892 my days were occupied, in
the various Colonies of Australasia, and in occasional visits to the New Hebrides, practically in the
same way as set forth again and again in the preceding Chapters. Colony after Colony, and Congregation
after Congregation listened with ever-deepening interest to the narrative of God's dealings with the
Islanders, and to the record of the effects produced by
my relating these incidents wherever my steps had
been led in the interests of Missionary Enterprise. If
I have accomplished nothing else by all these travels
and toils, this at least has been accomplished, and I
write it down to the praise of my blessed Redeemer—

23

there are Missionaries at this day laboring in every
Heathen Land, who have assured me that they first
gave themselves away to the glorious work, while
drinking in from my poor lips the living testimony
from the New Hebrides that the Gospel is still the
power of God and the wisdom of God unto Salvation;
and there are individual Christians, and sometimes
also Congregations of the Lord, now zealously supporting Missionaries to the Heathen in all the great
Mission fields of the world, who, till they heard the
story of Cannibals won for Christ by our noble Missionaries on the New Hebrides, had foolishly branded
the modern Christian Mission to the Heathen as the
greatest imposture and failure of the Century. God
has filled the ear and the eye of Christendom with the
story of one of the smallest, yet most fruitful, Missions
in one of the hardest and darkest fields on this Earth ;
and the whisper of "imposture" has died for shame,
while the arm of the scoffer falls paralyzed, and can no
longer sling its stones of abuse. "Failure" has been
blotted from the vocabulary of Missions and their
Critics by the Story of the New Hebrides.

But in 1892, events which had been maturing
through many years came to a crisis, the issue of
which was that I was sent a TOUR ROUND THE WORLD
in the Cause of Jesus, and for the sake of our beloved
Islanders. A broadly-drawn picture of these things,
without any attempt at details, seems all that is called
for here. This I now set myself to give to the patient
and indulgent reader of these pages, which after all

contain only brief and fragmentary scenes out of a crowded and hurried life.

The occasion was this : The sale of Intoxicants, Opium, Fire-Arms and Ammunition, by the Traders amongst the New Hebrideans, had become a terrible and intolerable evil. The lives of many Natives, and of not a few Europeans, were every year sacrificed in connection therewith, while the general demoralization produced on all around was painfully notorious. Alike in the Colonial and in the Home Newspapers, we exposed and condemned the fearful consequences of allowing such degrading and destructive agencies to be used as barter in dealing with these Islanders. It is infinitely sad to see the European and American Trader following fast in the wake of the Missionary with opium and rum! But, blessed be God, our Christian Natives have thus far, with very few exceptions, been able to keep away from the White Man's Fire-Water, that maddens and destroys. And not less cruel is it to scatter fire-arms and ammunition amongst Savages, who are at the same time to be primed with poisonous rum! This were surely Demons' work.

To her honor, be it said, that Great Britain prohibited all her own Traders, under heavy penalties, from bartering those dangerous and destructive articles in trade with the Natives. She also appealed to the other trading Nations, in Europe and America, to combine and make the prohibition " International," with regard to all the still unannexed Islands in the

Pacific Seas. At first America hesitated, owing to some notion that it was inconsistent with certain regulations for trading embraced in the Constitution of the United States. Then France, temporizing, professed willingness to accept the prohibition when America agreed. Thus the British Trader, with the Man-of-War and the High-Commissioner ready to enforce the laws against him, found himself placed at an overwhelming disadvantage, as against the neighboring Traders of every other Nationality, free to barter as they pleased. More especially so, when the things prohibited were the very articles which the masses of the Heathen chiefly coveted in exchange for their produce ; and where keen rivals in business were ever watchful to inform and to report against him. If illicit Trading prevailed, under such conditions, no one that knows average Human Nature can feel any surprise.

By-and-bye, the *Australian New Hebrides Company*, with two Steamers plying betwixt Sidney and the New Hebrides, took up the problem. Having planted Traders and Agents on the Islands, they found themselves handicapped in developing business, and began a brisk agitation in the Australasian and English Press, either to have the Prohibition applied all round, or completely rescinded. We have never accepted that alternative, but resolutely plead for an International Prohibitive law, as the only means under God to prevent the speedy sweeping off into Eternity of these most interesting Races by the tide of what is strangely styled Civilization.

At length Sir John Thurston, Her Majesty's High Commissioner for the Western Pacific, whose sympathies all through have been on our side, advised that the controversy in the Newspapers cease, and that our Missions and Churches send a deputation to America to win the assent of the United States. Consequently, the next Federal Assembly of the Australasian Presbyterian Churches instructed two of its Professors in the Divinity Hall of Victoria, who were then visiting Britain, to return by America, and do everything in their power to secure the adhesion of the United States Government to the International proposal. Lest, however, these Deputies found themselves unable to carry out their instructions, the same Assembly appointed me as Deputy, with identical instructions, to undertake the task during the succeeding year.

Meanwhile, the General Assembly of Victoria appointed the Rev. Professor Rentoul, D. D., Ormond College, the Rev. Jas. M'Gaw and myself, to represent them at the Pan-Presbyterian Council to be held at Toronto in September, 1892, and thus was I altogether unexpectedly launched on what proved to be the biggest of all my Missionary journeys. I received three several Commissions. But that from my own Church of Victoria, signed by the Moderator of the General Assembly and the Convener of our Foreign Mission Committee, bears most closely on the succeeding narrative. It set forth that, besides being appointed by the Federal Assembly to the Council at Toronto, I was empowered to use all legitimate influence with the Government of the United States " for the suppression of the trade in Fire-Arms, Intoxicating Liquors, and Opium, in the New Hebrides Islands and other unannexed Groups in the Western Pacific." I was also "authorized to procure two Missionaries to serve in the New Hebrides Islands under this Church," and to receive, on behalf of the Committee, " any contributions offered for its Foreign Missions." So that I acted, and had good right to act, in the name and by the authority of my own Church, and of the Federated Churches of Australasia.

With my Fellow-Deputies, and accompanied so far on the journey by my wife and our beloved daughter, we sailed from Sydney for San Francisco per s. s. *Monowai*, on 8th August, 1892. We had a very agreeable voyage, Captain Carey and all on board striving to make others happy. At Auckland, on the 13th, we had the great delight of spending a few hours with our very dear friends, Mr. and Mrs. Mackie, while the ship was discharging and receiving cargo and mails ; and, as she was leaving, several Ministers and other kind friends bade us Godspeed. Again, at Samoa, on the 18th, we had a few hours to spend, and were immensely gratified with the appearance of the Natives. They had a bright and healthy look as they came amongst the passengers with shells, operculums, and fans, their manner being characterized by a gentle

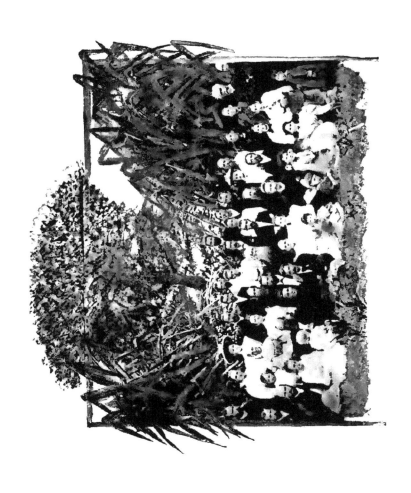

grace, that comes only with the coming of Christ into
a Savage man or woman. These, and the Raraton-
gans, and the people of Savage Islands, were amongst
the first whom the London Missionary Society saw
" flocking as the doves to their windows," from the
hordes of Cannibalism. They are tall, vigorous and
alert; and many of them are now teachers for Jesus,
and preachers of the Gospel in New Guinea and other
Heathen Islands. My heart overflows with love and
praise whenever I gaze on such trophies of Redeeming
Grace.

We reached Honolulu, the Hawaiian Capital, on the
25th, and spent nearly a whole day on shore. By a
circuitous drive, and on remarkably good roads, we
ascended a considerable hill and beheld the City spread
before us with its Palace, Government Buildings, Man-
sions and Villas. Large and beautiful trees surrounded
them all. Two Men-of-War and many other ships
swung at anchor in the harbor, and the shimmering
Sea completed a charming panorama. Smart and
diligent Chinese were at work on every hand, side by
side with the busy representatives of almost every
Nationality, eager to profit by the passing visitors.
The larger portion of the wharf seemed to be covered
with Bananas for San Francisco, the bunches carefully
bound up in dry leaves for shipping. I had never seen
so many in all my life thus gathered together.

The Queen had been deposed or deprived of power.
National interests were sacrificed in self-seeking and
partisanship. One could not but sigh for some strong

and righteous Government. They are a people capable
of great things. Everything seems to invite America
to annex the group; and it would be for the permanent welfare of all concerned.

On 2d September, we arrived at San Francisco,
after a delightful voyage. The society on board was
most congenial. We had happy daily Religious Services, and I managed to secure about eight hours to
myself out of every twenty-four for copying out translations, finishing my Dictionary of the Aniwan language, and other Mission work on which I was constantly engaged.

San Francisco is beautifully situated. Many of its
streets run up and down what seemed very steep hills,
and the principal highways are well supplied with
Electric Cars. Your own language is spoken, indeed,
but you feel at every turn, for all that, you are in a
Foreign City. On Sabbath morning, the first thing I
marked on leaving our Hotel was the joiners busy
with saw and plane, as on any other day ! The next
was a multitude of people flocking to a place of Public
Amusement, while others were going to Church. The
mass of the inhabitants were either in pursuit of pleasure, or following their usual avocations. Even the
City scavengers turned out with their carts, and were
cleaning the streets on the Lord's Day !

Yet we soon learned that even there the Lord Jesus
has many faithful servants living and working for His
glory. Several Ministers, hearing of our arrival,
found out our Hotel, and had us to assist them in their

Services. I delivered three Addresses, walking considerable distances between, and refusing to use public conveyances, or deprive man or beast of rest for my convenience,—to the great astonishment of my guides and friends.

On Monday morning we visited the famous Seal Rocks, a short distance from the city. There you see them, under protection, safely wobbling up on the rocks and basking contentedly in the sunshine, or tumbling delightedly into the Sea. From a considerable distance you hear the strange, half-barking sound of their voices, like muzzled dogs. From the plateau and promenade of a lovely private Garden near by and open to the public, we had a magnificent view of the Sea and all the surrounding scenery.

The same day, our whole party were invited to address a meeting of Lady Workers, who carry on a Mission in the Chinese quarter of the City. A report was given, and some Converts from the Flowery Land sang hymns to Jesus. It was joyful to see this spiritual life;—for tokens were not awanting of a darker and sadder picture all around us, in the dens of vice and misery.

Guided, but not very wisely, by Cook's representative, we left San Francisco on 5th September. Though now travelling night and day, we halted a few hours at the famous Mormon Settlement on 7th September. While looking at the grave of Brigham Young, a well-dressed old lady approached us and volunteered much information about her departed husband. He was one of the first settlers in the Salt Lake District, and had taken an active part in the building of the city and the Temple. She herself was a Mormon, and mourned that their glory was departing under the influence of the American laws. She was fervent in her defence of polygamy, but I noted that, with the Mormons as with the South Sea Savages, a separate house had to be provided for each wife! We saw their vast Temple, said to accommodate 15,000 persons, with tradesmen toiling busily to finish it, for the reception of Brigham Young on his speedy return to this Earth.

Replenishing our provision basket, as it was too expensive to take all our meals on board the train, our next run was to Chicago, which we reached on 10th September, and where we rested at a Hotel on the Sabbath Day. It was a day of tremendous storm and rain and no one of us ventured out even to Divine Service, especially as no Place of Worship was nigh at hand. Amongst our fellow-passengers from San Francisco had been a very kindly Christian man belonging to Chicago. He gave us every information, and on Monday showed us round the whole City by boat and car. We saw the Exhibition Buildings, lavishly expensive. The Horticultural Gardens were extensive and most interesting. In the Zoological Enclosure we saw a few remaining specimens of the Buffaloes, which once in myriads roamed the Prairies, but which Civilization has swept away.

Leaving Chicago, we arrived at Buffalo on the evening of the 13th September, and returned next day to

Niagara, whence by train and steamboat we were
bound for Toronto. We had already had a glimpse of
the Falls, where the train halted for a few minutes at a
convenient spot, and the view was grand! When next
I gazed on the spectacle, nigh at hand, I am afraid
almost to admit that I was rather disappointed. Too
transcendent expectations beforehand, I suppose!

I left Mrs. Paton and our daughter at the Falls for a
day, whilst I went on to Toronto to arrange for accommodation. What a blessing that I was guided to do so!
A great Agricultural Show was being held there; and,
on arriving in the evening, I found every Hotel and
Lodging so crowded that I walked till midnight from
one end of the City to the other, seeking in vain for a
bed. At last one manager of a Hotel proposed to
give me a " shake-down " in a Common Room, where
twenty-two were to sleep that same night. But the
Hotel-Keeper taking pity, and protesting that he could
not allow me to " tumble into that crowded place,"
gave me the address of a private family who took
in lodgers, to whom he commended me. With much
difficulty, at that late hour, I found the street and the
number. The owner, on hearing my appeal, said he
had already " turned away thirteen," and that he had
not a corner to receive me. I offered to pay him the
highest charges, " merely to rest in the Hall all
night," rather than to tramp the streets. Calling his
wife, he said: " I have not the heart to turn this old
man away! May he not sleep on the floor of our new
empty Room?" Her answer was: " I have neither

3

bed, nor bedclothes, nor even a pillow to give him."
But I was glad of the shelter over my head. A chair
was brought in and placed in the middle of the floor.
Kneeling, I thanked the Lord, and my hosts. Then,
utterly worn out, I placed my travelling handbag for a
pillow, rolled my clothes tightly round me, lay down,
and enjoyed a most refreshing sleep.

Next morning I found my way to the Presbyterian
Church Offices, where a cordial welcome awaited me,
and news of ample accommodation for our comfort, all
generously provided. Several invitations were pressed
on me, but I accepted that of Mrs. Park, who had in
the old days been a member of my Bible-class in the
Green Street Mission, Glasgow, and it was a great joy
to meet once more her sister and herself. The attention of many other friends was also very great, and
far too devoted, making us feel ashamed at the love
lavished on us.

At the Pan-Presbyterian Council I met and became
acquainted with representative Ministers and Laymen
from all parts of the world, but in specially large numbers from Canada and the United States. Along with
Fellow-Deputies, I addressed the Assembly on Foreign
Missions, and on the urgent reasons for my present
visit to America. A Minister from the United States at
once rose and protested that there must be some mistake, that it was " an insult to their honor " to insinuate
that they declined to join with Britain in such an International Prohibition ! I repeated my statements,
showed my Commission, and affirmed that it was

certainly as I had represented. He telegraphed to
the Authorities at Washington, and next day he
courageously stood up in his place and admitted that
he was wrong, and that I had correctly stated the
facts. The action of that good and brave man, once
for all, made the issue plain and cleared my future
course.

I was proud of our Professor Rentoul, of Ormond
College. He at once took a leading place in the
Council. In wisdom, in vast learning, and in eloquent
debate, he was the equal of the best men from all
Presbyterian Christendom. I envied the Students
who sit at the feet of such a noble Master in the
School of Christ.

In response to my appeals, Ministers from Canada
and the United States began informing me how many
collections they had given "for the New Hebrides
Mission," and subscriptions "for building the new
Mission Ship." I had never heard of these, and in-
quired to whom they had been given. They replied
that it was my "alternate," commissioned from the
Presbyterian Church of Victoria! I assured them that
my Church appointed no alternate, and that this person must be an impostor. A Committee was appointed to look into the matter. The eloquent
pleader turned out to be a Roman Catholic student
who had joined the Victorian Church, had been
licensed and ordained as a Minister, had broken down
in character, and disappeared from the Colony. Now,
under a false name and forged credentials, represent-

ing himself as a Minister in full and honorable stand-
ing, and a Missionary who had been thirteen years in
the New Hebrides, he was raising large sums of
money ostensibly for our Mission, but applying it all
to his own uses. His lectures were cleverly com-
pounded out of my *Autobiography*, with wild adorn-
ments and fancies of his own. He had Collecting
Cards for children and for adults, the minimum subscription on the latter being half-a-dollar! His New
Ship was to be sheathed in brass, and every subscriber
of not less than $5 was to have his name engraved
thereon! One man informed us of giving $25 to have
his Family Register completed on the sheath of brass!

Dr. Rentoul, by appointment, officially exposed and
denounced this impostor on the floor of the Council.
But, in these vast countries, a lie is hard to overtake
and to extinguish. Letters continued to reach me
from many quarters, and urgent appeals that I should
sanction his arrest. At one place he drank for a week,
after a series of Mission Meetings. The Ministers of
Buffalo at length caused him to be arrested; and the
Public Attorney, founding on his so-called credentials
as my assistant, summoned me to appear before the
Grand Jury at his trial. In a "blizzard," I travelled
two nights and a day—one night the severest and
coldest I ever endured—and reached my destination in
time.

Having answered all questions by the Attorney and
the Grand Jury, they asked me to see the prisoner,
and testify whether he was the ex-Priest Riordan, now

giving his name as Ruthven. I thereon handed the Attorney a pamphlet exposing the evils and errors of Popery, being three Lectures by V. H. Riordan, with his portrait on the front page. They all at once recognized him by this likeness. Nevertheless, I was enjoined to go and see him, and report what took place. He was behind an iron-grated door, and two ladies were conversing with him from without. Addressing him at once by his name, I said: " It grieves me to see you here in these circumstances, Mr. Riordan." Completely off his guard, he at once answered to his own name, and addressed me by mine: " And I am very sorry, Dr. Paton, to be here in such circumstances." This was enough! I reported what transpired, and the Jury took a hearty laugh at the simplicity of the interview. I was dismissed for the time.

In answer to the Prosecutor, he explained that when he renounced the errors of Popery, he assumed his mother's name for life—Ruthven ; yet there they had his own pamphlet, with his real name, printed in Philadelphia less than two years before ! Being committed for trial before the Supreme Court, he spent his time of waiting in abusing me from his cell through the pages of a Sunday newspaper, as " a drunkard " debauching my Sacred Office, and " a hireling " living by commission on the moneys raised for the Mission. So madly did he rage, that some suspected he was put up to do so, in order that his agent might work up a plea of insanity, if the case at last went against him.

At his trial, which occupied the greater part of three days, I was again cited to appear. The Jury found him "guilty," but strangely enough recommended him to mercy, and his lawyer pled for a money fine as the penalty. The Judge sternly refused. He had been found guilty in every count. His sentence would be "twelve months in prison with hard labor." That was "extreme leniency." It should have been "three years."

One would have thought that this should have extinguished him. But no! His imprisonment has expired. He is again at his lecturing and lying. Quite lately I saw a report of his appearing at a place called Dunmore. The Romanists mobbed him. In reply to their eggs and snowballs he fired a pistol into the crowd. The cry then rose, "Lynch the Renegade!" Ruthven, bounding through an open door, scaling fences, and crossing lots, managed to escape. But a warrant was at once issued for his apprehension, and doubtless he is proving the truth of one text, which he has listened to in vain : "The way of transgressors is hard."

During the Pan-Presbyterian Council, I addressed many meetings in the churches of Toronto and its suburbs, receiving, on one occasion, by the kindness of Dr. Parsons, a collection of two hundred dollars for our Mission. And, by the urgent request of many Ministers, I spent a considerable time after the Council in visiting the chief towns of Ontario, where I was cordially received everywhere, and had very great pleasure throughout the whole circuit.

Never, since I left the Christian Islands on the New Hebrides, such as Aniwa and Aneityum, have I seen the Sabbath Day kept so well, and the Churches so largely attended, as at Toronto and in the chief towns of Ontario. In that Capital, the Public-Houses are closed from seven o'clock on Saturday night till eight o'clock on Monday morning. No confectioners, tobacconists, fruiterers, or the like, are open on the Lord's Day. The street Electric Car, and the Omnibus are at rest. All workmen are enjoying their Sabbath privilege, like other Citizens. And all this is carried through by the will of the People themselves, and by the vigilance and influence of the servants of God. Surely, men of Christian principle, of grit, and of public spirit, could, by keeping their hand on the helm, secure in the same way the blessed Day of Rest for all, in every City throughout the Christian World.

By cordial invitations from many men of the highest rank in the Church of God throughout the States, I was pressed to occupy their Pulpits, and tell the story of our Mission to the Cannibals of the New Hebrides. They also formed a Committee of their own number to advise and help me in promoting the prohibition against trading with the Natives in Intoxicants and Fire-Arms. And the great-hearted Dr. John Hall, in order to give me a good start in New York, offered me his Pulpit for my first Sabbath there.

On the way, I had promised to spend an afternoon

and evening at Rochester, with the Rev. Principal
Osgood of the Baptist College. An extraordinary
spirit of consecration seemed to rest on Professors and
Students alike. My heart was overflowing with joy,
to think of the type of Ministers and Missionaries certain to go forth from such a Home of Piety and of
Learning.

Never can I express how much I owe to the genuine
and brotherly friendship of Dr. Sommerville of New
York, and his devoted lady. Not simply did they
make their House my very Home, whensoever I chose
to return to it, but they heaped on me every token of
consideration and of helpful sympathy. Amidst his
many cares, as a Minister of the Covenanting Church,
and his literary labors, as Editor of the *Herald of
Mission News*, he became Honorary Treasurer for me
in the States, and according to his utmost ability
opened up all my way, and helped me at every turn.
They are forever my dearly beloved friends in the
bonds of Jesus Christ.

After my first two Sabbaths in New York, one in
Dr. John Hall's Church, and one in Dr. Sommerville's,
I had no difficulty in arranging for as much work,
Sunday and Saturday alike, as my strength could overtake. One lady, who heard me in Dr. Hall's, sent me
one thousand dollars, as from " Elizabeth Jane." In
addressing the Chamber of Commerce, the Doctor
himself announced clearly the special object of my
visit to America, and described the features of our
Mission. This, being fully reported in the Public

Press, woke a widespread interest, and invitations poured in upon me from all branches of the Church, excepting only the Romish and the Unitarian.

The way to Washington, and to influence with the Governing Authorities, was prepared for me thus. Being a stranger and only a poor Missionary, I asked every Public Meeting, held on any day except Sabbath, to forward a Petition to the President and the Congress, signed by the Chairman, in favor of the Prohibition of Intoxicants and Fire-Arms, as barter by American Traders on the New Hebrides, or other un-annexed Islands in the Pacific. The Daily Press reported all these Petitions. The Public became thoroughly interested. And even the Authorities were expecting my appeal in person. Nay, I cannot but regard it as of the Lord that my first Sabbath in Washington happened to be in the pulpit of Dr. Bartlet, where I, altogether unknown to myself, was pleading the cause before the Chief Secretary of the Government. He sent me fifty dollars for the Mission, invited me to lunch with his family, and gave me ample opportunity, by answers to many questions, to state all the case, and to deepen all round the growing interest in our Mission.

On the forenoon of the following Sabbath, I occupied the pulpit of Dr. Hamlin, and the President of the United States heard my story and appeal. Many Senators and Members of Congress, having matters thus rehearsed, were able to weigh the question carefully, before I made my official statement at all. The

President declared himself quite frankly to be deeply interested, and willing to expedite in every possible way the negotiations with Britain. It emerged that in the British reply there was a new clause, empowering one of the contracting parties to license Traders, under certain circumstances, to sell Intoxicating Drinks. The President struck his pen through that clause, and at once returned it, insisting on its excision. Had Britain agreed to this, President Harrison would then have signed the Treaty. But, alas, week after week elapsed, and no reply came. A new Election took effect, and President Cleveland was installed at the White House.

My Advisory Committee in America now insisted that I must wait till the new Government's arrangements were all completed, and once more press my appeal. I resumed my work of addressing Public Meetings every week day, and Congregations every Sabbath Day, always sending, from the former, Petitions to the President and Congress regarding the proposed Prohibition on the Islands. I had also private interviews with many leading Politicians. To all I pointed out that, as America was now united with Britain in the Dual Protectorate of Fiji, we only sought the extension of prohibition on that Group to the Group of the New Hebrides.

Constantly engaged in these Mission interests, I planned my second visit to Washington to take place at the same time as the General Assembly of the Presbyterian Church of the United States. I had the

honor to address it on Foreign Missions, and to preach
before a number of Congregations during its sittings,
for a very deep interest was manifested in the won-
drous workings of God on the New Hebrides.

I was introduced to the new President, when the
General Assembly went in procession to do him honor.
Both he and Mrs. Cleveland welcomed me to America,
and, a few days after, they invited me to lunch at the
White House, privately, that they might question me
freely regarding the Islanders and our work. They both
seemed to me to be genuine followers of the Saviour,
and sincerely interested in the salvation of the Heathen
World.

The Presbyterian Assembly thereafter appointed a
large Deputation of its leading men to accompany me
in laying officially before the Government our griev-
ance regarding Fire-Arms and Intoxicants, and pleading that the United States should unite with Britain in
the Prohibition of all trading with Natives in the same.
In order to save time, and secure lucidity, Professor
Hodge carefully prepared and read our statement.
The President expressed himself as deeply interested,
and requested the document to be left with him for
reference. We anxiously awaited the result; but the
final reply from Britain was still delayed. Our hearts
grew sore with hope deferred!

In course of time I was informed at the British
Colonial Office in London, that as France and Russia
had withdrawn from the proposal, the negotiations
were for the present suspended. France, for years,

postured before the world as ready to enforce this prohibition, if America would; and now, when America
was ready, France withdrew! Still, on the highest of
all moral grounds, let us plead with America, Ger-
many, and Britain, already united in their triple Protectorate of Samoa, to extend the same prohibition to
the New Hebrides, and the other unannexed Islands
in the Western Pacific. If they would do so, the
other Powers interested could scarcely fail to agree,
and France would be ashamed to stand before the
world as the only Civilized Nation, exploiting the
bodies and souls of poor Savages by trading with
them in Fire-Arms and Drink for mere godless greed
of gold.

In Boston, the Ministers of all the Reformed
Churches, having formed a representative Committee,
organized a series of meetings, and cordially invited me
to address them. Dr. Joseph Cook and his gifted
wife gave me a public reception, to which many of the
leading Citizens, as well as Professional men, were invited, and where I answered all sorts of questions regarding Missions in general, and the New Hebrides in
particular. I was also twice introduced to the audiences at his famous Monday Lectures; and my
replies to testing problems, there submitted, were
printed in *Our Day*, and woke not a little interest in
the work of God amongst the Cannibals of the
Southern Seas. To all these generous friends at
Boston, I am forever indebted, but very specially to
John Gilchrist, Esq., an office-bearer in the Presby-

terian Church, who toiled in the cause incessantly, and whom may the Lord Jesus richly recompense!

One curious experience befell me there, outside the range of my ordinary work. A "Temperance Union" of Women engaged me to address a Working Folks' Meeting on a Sabbath afternoon, in what they called the Peoples' Church. When I arrived, nearly half of the large Platform was occupied with ladies scraping away and tuning their violins, large and small! A lady occupied the chair, and introduced Dr. Blank, a Unitarian or rather an Infidel, who was to speak for ten minutes, and then leave the meeting in my hands. He knew that I had to leave within an hour, and drive to another meeting, but he went on and on, tracing a Carpenter all through his life to exhausted old age, manifestly stirring up class against class, and sowing the seeds of infidelity. At last, he wound up by picturing the Carpenter, outworn and ready to die, sitting with his wife and children around the table at their evening meal, taking the bread and breaking it and saying: "Eat ye all of it, for this is my body broken for you; this do in remembrance of me, for I have worn out my life for your sakes." Whereon, his wife poured out the tea, and said: "If the bread is your body broken for us, this tea is my blood shed for you; drink ye all of it in remembrance of me, as I have spent my life in toiling for you."

Being able to stand it no longer, I turned to the ladies behind us and said aloud: "Who is this blasphemer that you have set up to speak to the people?

He is simply belching out Infidelity, and setting man
against man. This is a black disgrace to you all!"
He paused a moment, and then said: "I wish this
Congregation to understand that, in what I have just
said about the Carpenter and his bread, I throw no slight
on the name or memory of one who thus parted from
his followers long ago"—and thereon he resumed his
seat, having spoken for nearly the whole hour. Reply
was impossible for lack of time, and my expected
Address was crushed aside. But, ere I left the Platform, I uttered a few burning words, and the whole
audience seemed to go with me. I denounced all setting of the poor against the rich, as alien to the spirit
of Jesus. I branded as an insult to the Divine Saviour
of the world the blasphemer's parody of the Lord's
Supper, to which we had been treated. I warned these
Temperance workers that, in bringing such a teacher
of Abstinence before the people, they were degrading
the cause which they desired to promote. And finally,
I summoned them to remember that we must all
appear before the Judgment Seat of Christ, and implored them, and Dr. Blank amongst the rest, to seek
pardon and acceptance at the feet of Jesus now, that
they might find their Judge was also their Saviour in
the last awful day! A hasty Benediction was pronounced, at the Chairwoman's request. I hurried from
the Church, greatly shocked, but encouraged by the
handshake and the "God bless you!" of many whom
I passed. There was one small consolation which I

unfeignedly enjoyed—the fiddling ladies had no opportunity of displaying their skill on that Lord's Day!

While I was in America many minds were being troubled with ideas regarding what is styled the "Second Probation." At one of his famous Monday Lectures, Dr. Joseph Cook put to me, on the Platform, the following amongst other questions: "How would Missionaries, teaching the Second Probation, succeed with the Cannibals on your Island?" My reply was: "How can they succeed on such terms anywhere? Our Cannibals would say,—If we have a second chance hereafter, let us enjoy our present pleasures and risk the future!" Again he asked: "How would Missionaries holding that doctrine, but promising not to teach it, succeed amongst them?" I replied: "Hypocrites are a poor set everywhere, but especially in the Mission Field. How could a man succeed in teaching what he did not believe? Cannibals, like Children, are quick to discern insincerity; and such a man could do no good, but only evil amongst them." Joseph Cook and his like-minded wife appeared to be noble instruments in the hand of God, for the defence of truth and righteousness.

During this supplementary series of Meetings I happened to reach Chicago during the Great Exhibition. Dr. Macpherson greatly helped me, and arranged all my work. The City was crowded with visitors from all the World. There were many things in the Big Show that one would have liked to see; but when I learned how its Directors, in violation of their agreement with the Government, opened it on Sabbath, and turned the Lord's Day into a Saturnalia of sports and amusements, I positively declined to enter within its gates. They made a huge noise about accommodating the working men, but they really sought mere selfish gains. They filled the streets with advertising cars, with flags flying from each, announcing their theatres and shows, desecrating the Holy Day. Thank God such Heaven-defying conduct was condemned from many a Protestant Pulpit, and the Congregations warned against countenancing such a sinful and shameful Vanity Fair !

The Directors, having secured President Cleveland to open the Exhibition, desired him to go from Washington by special train on the Sabbath Day. Their plan was to utilize the occasion by enormous Excursions from all quarters on the Day of Rest. But the God-fearing Presbyterian President went with a usual train on Saturday, took up his residence at a Private Hotel, and showed his disapproval of their tactics by declining their projected ovation. On Sabbath morning he attended worship at Dr. Macpherson's Church. A Baptismal Service was intimated for the afternoon. The President again attended. He opened the Exhibition officially, but left the City as privately as he had come to it, and this rebuke was not misunderstood by the Community, and was greatly appreciated by decided Christians, to whom the rest of the Day of God is a Heavenly heritage for all the creatures of Earth, which no man may lawfully alienate or impair.

To a man like myself, the results brought a certain retributive joy. The rush of Foreigners, after the first two or three Sabbaths, was soon over. Then it was discovered that the masses of the Working People of Chicago absented themselves on the Lord's Day, knowing well that it was not for their benefit that this thing was done, but merely to coin money out of them. Finding that, instead of a gain, the opening on the Sabbath was a deadly loss, the Managers proposed to close it, but found themselves tied hand and foot by their own past action at law. Conspicuously, the City suffered through the vices and crimes thereby fostered; and will continue to suffer; for such evil cannot be swept away with the temporary buildings of the Exhibition. Doom seemed to overtake the authors speedily. One of the leaders was cruelly shot; and the gates were at last closed in silence, and apparently in shame !

Very varied were the means adopted, by interested friends, to arrest attention on the New Hebrides, and create enthusiasm in their cause. One very memorable occasion was at Pittsburg, where J. I. Buchanan, Esq., gave a great dinner, to which he invited the Owners and Editors of all the local Newspapers, to meet the New Hebrides Missionary. After I had addressed them, they tackled me with questions regarding the Islanders, and on all conceivable aspects of work for Christ amongst Cannibals. Most of them got deeply interested; and, next day, the whole Press of the City was full of the Mission, and of the reasons for our seeking

4

the Prohibition of Fire-Arms and Intoxicants as articles of trade amongst the Natives.

I had now visited the leading Towns in all the Northern States, and not a few on the borders of some of the Southern States, being everywhere received by Ministers and People with exceeding kindness and exceptional liberality. My next anxiety was to be present at the Assembly of the Canadian Presbyterian Church, and I therefore decided to leave the work undone, which was daily being pressed upon me throughout the States, and to hasten thither. This was surely of God's guidance; at least I reverently think so; for I reached the Assembly Hall, all unknown to myself, on the night of their Foreign Mission Report; and the first thing I heard was an " Overture " from Nova Scotia, urging the Assembly to hand over their three Missionaries on the New Hebrides to the Australian Churches, which were now " both able and willing to support them "!

The Assembly received me very cordially. The Moderator invited me to speak immediately after the Overture had been presented. I conveyed to them the greetings of our Church, and of our Synod on the Islands, and reported in general terms on the Home and Foreign Missions in Australasia. Then I turned to the Moderator, and asked on whose authority it was declared that the Australian Churches were both able and willing to take over the Nova Scotian Mission on the New Hebrides, with its annual cost of about £1300. The question was put to the Assembly.

There was a significant silence for several moments, and then some one feebly replied: "On Dr. Geddie's." I retorted, that surely the author of the Overture was ashamed of it, when he sought to palm it on the honored father of our Mission, now many years resting in his grave! I demonstrated, by irrefragable facts and figures, that the Australian Churches were in no position to undertake this additional expense; and, further, I insisted that to give up this specially-honored Mission would be one of the greatest losses to the spiritual life of their own Congregations and Sabbath Schools. It was the Mother of all their Missions! It was the Mission which had awakened in them all the Missionary spirit they now possessed!

The Moderator emphatically protested, from the Chair, that he hoped the General Assembly "would hear no more of such a proposal." Yet the agitation is carried on, from what creditable motive it is very hard to see. The Editor of their *Mission Record*, with a few men of similar spirit at his back, seems to have determined to cut the connection betwixt Nova Scotia and the New Hebrides, and to close by violence one of the noblest chapters in that Church's history. They have written to the Australian Churches on the matter, and I venture to predict that their answers will be more emphatic than even my instantaneous protest. The nobler spirits in Nova Scotia ought to squelch out this miserable agitation, which is killing the Missionary enthusiasm and curtailing the liberality of their Church.

Surrounded by a multitude of devoted Ministers and

Elders, I agreed to remain two months in Canada, and address as many Meetings every day of the week as could possibly be crowded into time and space. To relieve the pressure on Mission Funds in Nova Scotia, I offered to give up twenty days entirely to them, with all the proceeds from every Meeting. They received, I understand, above £500; and I trust that by my Addresses, one at least every day and four or five every Sabbath, all the Funds of all these Congregations prospered and continue to prosper; for I humbly and gratefully recognize the fact that God has used me not for one Mission but for all Missions, and not through one Church but through all His Churches.

The series of Meetings, up to Quebec, was mapped out at the Assembly, and the whole of the arrangements were entrusted to the Rev. J. W. Mitchell of Thorold, a man of deep devotion and of untiring zeal. Our Treasurer was A. K. Macdonald, Esq., Toronto, to whose kindness also we were profoundly indebted. Countless applications poured in upon us. It was no uncommon thing to address two or even three Meetings daily, and to travel long distances between them by conveyance and rail. On Sunday we delivered never less than three Addresses, but more frequently five, and sometimes even seven, including the Bible Classes and Sabbath Schools. It was dreadfully exhausting work. Sometimes I hesitated, fearing every day would be my last. But again my vigor returned, and my heart hungered to overtake all that I possibly could, knowing that the time was short. Besides, in

this tour as always, the getting of Collections, however
anxiously desired for our Mission, was never my pri-
mary aim; but always the saving of souls, by the
story of the New Hebrides. For that cause I would
gladly die. But I did not die; and there was given a
new illustration of the meaning of that inspired saying
—"The joy of the Lord is your strength"—the work,
which is our *joy*, uplifts rather than oppresses us!

The incidents of these journeys would fill a goodly
volume. But I had neither the leisure nor the inclina-
tion to record them day by day. One or two specially
impressed themselves on my memory, however, and
may here be glanced at.

On one occasion, after a long Railway ride, I found
myself set down on the wrong side of a flooded River,
the bridge having been swept away. The Station-
Master pointed us to a boat, kept by a farmer, which,
if we reached, might ferry us over. But two huge
fields betwixt us and the spot were flooded with the
overflow, and these had to be crossed. A young lady,
a gentleman, and I, all equally eager to get to the
other side, resolved to try. We waded to the Boat-
Landing, and reached it in a very bedraggled state.
There the boat had been left, awaiting some one's return, but the farmer was across the River. None of
us felt very brave about the experiment of rowing
across the racing current! Our fellow traveller, nevertheless, resolved to try. Minimizing my warning
about rowing a long way up in the quieter water, and
then slanting across with the sweep of the current, he

went up only a little, and quickly plunged in. His boat was whirled away like a cork. We held our breath, while the young farmer on the opposite bank kept shouting and gesticulating, running down the River, and guiding the rower as best he could. It was with a sigh of thankful relief that we saw the traveller stand up at last on the farther side, safe but badly shaken.

The farmer now took the oars in hand, and with his great strength and greater skill ferried first one and then the other across in safety, but not without peril. In a high light cart he mounted us and bore us securely across another field, through three feet of water if not more, and planted us gladly at his fireside. There the lady waited, that her dripping clothes might be dried, and the other traveller found his way to his desired haven. But, the hour of my Meeting having already arrived, I hastened to address them, with clothes soaked through and through, and was immediately thereafter driven to another town at a distance of several miles. Without any opportunity of proper re-freshment, or of getting clothes dried or changed, I spoke for an hour and a half to a large Public Meeting there, and then retired for the night. My clothes were hung up to dry. I had to start by train very early next morning. When I dressed, the damp of yester-day's drenching still hung about them, and made me shiver. For two days my bones and muscles felt very sore, and the dread of severe rheumatic fever hung over me. But I sustained myself with the assurance that the Great Physician would take care of me, since none of this had been brought on by selfish pleasure, or self-willed obstinacy, but in devotion to His Will and in doing His work. I suffered no further harm, and carried through all the Meetings, praising Jesus my Saviour.

On another occasion I was for a time seriously perplexed. A kind Minister drove me, after conducting several Meetings under his charge, to join the Night Train at a lonely crossing. Arrangements had been made at Headquarters to set me down, pick me up, and set me down again at such places, in order to reach certain Meetings, and thence go on my way to others, with the least possible loss of time. Being duly despatched by my friend, I was set down, in the darkness, at such a crossing, where was neither sight of any house, nor sound of any human being. The Guard, in manifest pity, exclaimed, " I don't know, sir, what you can do here! I am extremely sorry to leave you. But, for God's sake, keep off the line. The Express follows. The rails are wet, and you might never hear her! Some one will surely meet you. Good-bye!"

His Train soon disappeared into the darkness. I tried to rest, sitting on my travelling bag, but it was too cold, and rain began to fall. Marching about to keep up the circulation, I kept hallooing as loudly as I could every few moments, but no sound came in reply. Worn out and greatly disheartened, I at last put both hands to my mouth and began the Australian

Koo-ee! Koo-ee! and sustained it with all the breath
and strength I possessed. By-and-bye, in the pauses,
I heard a faint and far reply, like the echo of my own
voice. It drew nearer and nearer in response to my
cry, and at last grew into the salutation of a glad human voice. It was the Minister, appointed to meet
me, who now emerged out of the darkness. There
were two crossings in the district, and they had left me
at the wrong one! He had tied his horse to the fence,
and followed my cries through the night. We stum-
bled our way back, and were ere long welcomed to his
cozy Manse; and I tucked myself into a warm bed
as soon as possible. Not without praising our Heavenly Guide, I soon fell into a deep and sweet sleep,
and felt able next Sabbath morning for any amount of
Meetings. The Holy Day proved to be exceptionally
busy, and exceptionally happy ; for I was with a good
and true Minister of Jesus Christ, and that transforms
all work into joyful fellowship.

Once the shaft of our engine broke, and the train
stood still. The Guard advised all the passengers to
leave and take to the fields across the fence. I decided to stick by the train. A messenger started on
the rails behind and another in front, and each ran
with all his might, waving the red flag and shouting.
But the Engineers never lost their heads for a moment.
They screwed and hammered and chiselled; they un-
loosed one part and pitched it up among the coals;
they fixed and adjusted another, in the most mys-
terious ways, as it seemed to me. And in a very short

time, to the delight and amazement of all, that train
began to move slowly ahead, and crept on steadily to
the nearest Station, one side of the engine only being
in working order. The alarm of all was very great, as
an Express was due behind us and might any moment have crashed upon the scene. "Our Father
knoweth."

At another time I was travelling, by rail, a great
distance to address a Mid-Day Meeting. Only one
hour was free, and then I must join another train.
Two or three Stations before reaching the former destination, a gentleman surprised me, exclaiming, "Dr.
Paton, here is your Lunch! You will not have a
minute for food either before or after the Meeting.
Leave the jug and plates at any Station, and they will
be returned. Good-bye and God bless you!" I
looked on this excellent meal with very curious sen-
sations, as if it had dropped to me out of the Hand
that feeds the ravens; and I prayed my Saviour to
bless the good-hearted giver.

I may here record that this period of my life was
fuller of constant stir and excitement, rushing from
Meeting to Meeting, and from Town to Town, than
any other through which, heretofore, I had ever
passed, without one single day of rest, or almost an
hour of breathing space. I do not think it is exagger-
ation to say that, on an average, during these months,
I must have addressed ten Meetings on the ordinary
days of the week and five every Sunday. I certainly
know that, during many special weeks, the numbers

far exceeded these. Blessed be God, who so marvel-
lously sustained me through it all. When my throat
got a little husky, my only medicine was a sip of pure
Glycerine, a little bottle of which I always carried with
me. My daily diet was always, by choice, the simplest
and homeliest food which I could obtain—a plate of
porridge with milk, a cup of tea with bread and butter,
and a very moderate amount of flesh meat of any
kind, often for days together none at all. And my
only stimulant was—the ever-springing fountain of
pure joy in the work of my Lord and Saviour Jesus
Christ!

One thing was at first a great worry to me, but at
length solved itself very happily. I cannot, with any
conscience, use cars, cabs, trains, or steamboats on the
Lord's Day, except under such an emergency of
" necessity or mercy," that my Lord, if He met me on
the way, would declare me "blameless." On beginning in America, it was enforced on me from every
quarter that I must use these conveyances on the
Sabbath, owing to enormous distances, or find my
mission an utter failure. My one answer was: " No
working man or woman shall ever accuse me at the
Bar of God for needlessly depriving them of their Day
of Rest, and imperilling or destroying their highest
welfare." Shoulders were shrugged knowingly, heads
shaken rather pityingly, and gentle appeals made to
yield for the sake of the higher interests of the Mission.
But I held my ground unfalteringly. It became known
that I would not use such conveyances, and that I

HEATHEN NATIVES OF AMBRIM.
Heads and faces of women are covered with lime as sign of mourning.

MEMORIALS OF THE DEAD, AMBRIM.
Stone Altar in front is one on which pigs are killed.

sturdily trudged from Meeting to Meeting on foot, all through the Lord's day. Immediately the private carriages of friends of Jesus and His Mission were placed largely at our disposal; and, in all cases, I pled for such arrangements as gave the horse its rest, and the man his opportunity of worship. Whensoever I was necessitated to hire for the Lord's Day, it was invariably so planned that not only was proper food duly provided for man and beast, but the driver was invited and encouraged to join the Service of the House of God. I pray my Lord to accept my lifelong testimony and practice on this supremely important matter, and to use it for the preservation of the blessed Day of Rest as the inalienable heritage of all His toiling creatures,—next to the gift of His own Son, one of the most priceless of all His boons to the Human Race!

The time had come that I must say farewell to Canada and the States. It was the first time I had ever seen these new and marvellous Lands. My soul was not unaware of their beauties, nor unresponsive to their grandeur of scenery. But my whole time and strength were otherwise required; and I turned not aside from the call of my Lord. He knows that my heart rejoices in all the wonders of His Power, not the less that I spend myself in proclaiming the greater wonders of His Grace. All my recollections of intercourse with the Ministers and the People of the New World are abidingly sweet, and move me to bless the Lord for the God-fearing, Bible-loving, and Sabbath-keeping Nations that have sprung from our British Race. From the highest to the humblest they received me with royal welcome, and heard me with loyal sympathy. Their help was generous, and was gladly given. Their interest in the work of God was genuine, and was frankly displayed. And their delight in listening to the story of the salvation of the South Sea Cannibals, made me firm in the assurance that they themselves already know within their own souls the unspeakable worth of Jesus!

CHAPTER II.

THE HOME-LANDS AND THE ISLANDS.

A.D. 1894—1897. ÆT. 70—73.

.

CHAPTER II.

THE HOME-LANDS AND THE ISLANDS.

A.D. 1894—1897. ÆT. 70—73.

Arrival in Great Britain.—Requisitions.—Professors and Students.—*Dayspring* Scheme.—Ten Years' Delay.—Gideon's Fleece Experiment.—Two Memorable Checks.—The " John G. Paton Mission Fund."—The *Dayspring* Disaster.—Mission Work on all the Islands.

I EMBARKED from New York for Liverpool, per the new and magnificent s. s. *Campania*. The vibrations of that vessel were more fearful than anything I had ever experienced in all my travels. There was some defect, which I hear has since been remedied. I was scarcely conscious of ever sleeping at all, and the ship seemed to be constantly on the eve of shaking herself into fragments ! On the voyage I made the acquaintance of very dear friends, bearing my own name ; whose Home at Liverpool by-and-bye received me lovingly ; and where also I met the learned and honored Principal Paton of Nottingham.

My arrival in Britain revealed to me, immediately and amazingly, how times had changed since my previous visit, only ten years before. *Then* I had many difficulties to face in arranging for public meetings, especially in England, as set forth in a previous Chap-

ter. Many a weary day's tramping I had, even in
Scotland where something was known about the Mission to the New Hebrides, passing from Minister to
Minister, and pleading, frequently all in vain, for the
use of their Pulpits and for access to their Congregations. But since then, by my brother's insistence, the
story of my life had gone through the Land in my
Autobiography. I was no longer treated as a stranger,
but as the dearly beloved friend of every one who had
read my book. Blessed be God, who used it for His
glory, and gave our Mission appeal everywhere an
open door, such as never in my most hopeful hours
had my faith even dreamed!

Now, hundreds of invitations poured in on my
British Committee, all Honorary Helpers who grudged
no amount of labor and pains. I found a Series of
Meetings already arranged for me, covering the principal towns and cities of the United Kingdom,—Mr.
Watson of Belfast taking charge in Ireland, Mr.
Langridge in England, and my brother James, with
his Honorary Secretary, arranging for Scotland, and
acting as General Director of the Mission. When
those had been fairly overtaken, the additional applications had risen to several hundreds more than could
possibly be faced, unless I prolonged my stay for
years. My Committee at one time found themselves
dealing with a mass of 500 invitations! A selection
had to be made of the more important and populous
centres for the Services on the Lord's Day, and one or
two Meetings each day during the week in the smaller

surrounding towns ; but even then the disappointments were many and grievous; and not more so to them than to me ; for I did passionately desire to tell every human being the story of the Gospel on the New Hebrides, that other and still other souls might be won thereby for Jesus my Lord.

One very precious feature of my tour was this :—the manner in which Ministers and Christian workers of all the Churches united to welcome me, and gave very practical support to this Presbyterian Mission. Frequently, the invitation was signed by all the Ministers of the district, excepting only the Roman Catholic ; and my prayers rose daily to my Lord that my humble presence might be one of the means in His loving hand of paving the way for a closer union amongst the Members of His Redeemed Flock. I was much touched by the requisition that came to me from my well-beloved Dumfries, with the names of all the Ministers, and full of tender references to my early associations with the Queen of the South, as in our boyhood we loved to call her !

The Congregations, on week days not less than on Sabbaths, filled the largest Public Halls and Churches in each locality ; with frequent overflow Meetings at which I had to speak for fifteen minutes or so, and then leave them in the hands of others, whilst I drove or ran to the principal Meeting, now opened and awaiting my Address. During the two years of my Tour, I addressed very nearly 1400 audiences, ranging from a few hundreds to five and six thousand each,

5

and in doing so I travelled over many thousands of miles, on foot and in every kind of conveyance that is used in the English-speaking world.

The Chairmen at my various Meetings represented every type of Christian worker, and all social grades, from the godly Tradesman, evangelizing in his quiet Mission Hall, up through Ministers and Mayors, Provosts and Members of Parliament, Bishops and Archbishops, to Lords and Dukes and other Peers of the Realm. Under this rush of the Missionary Spirit, many conventional barriers were broken down, so that I was, even on Sunday, invited to give my Address from the very Pulpit in Episcopal Churches, as for example in the Pro-Cathedral at Manchester. On week days, this was a not infrequent experience.

These things, and all my opportunities of usefulness, thus unexpectedly thrust upon me, at the close of a long life of toil and self-denial and sacrifice for Jesus, I devoutly laid at His feet, and implored Him to use me only for His glory. And I can truly say that I never felt more deeply humbled, all my days, than at the close of some of those almost unparalleled Missionary Meetings, when I was alone with my Saviour after all was over, and thinking of my lowly Home and all the way by which the God of my father had led me, from these hours of hardship to this day of triumph. Fame and influence laid me lower and lower yet, at the feet of Jesus, to whose grace alone everything was due.

Never were these feelings more present with me than when I was called upon to tell the story of our

Mission before the learned Professors and eager
Students, at so many Universities, Colleges, Theolog-
ical Halls, and similar Institutes. I have a note of at
least sixty-three Seats of Learning, including Princeton
and the most famous Colleges in America, as well as
Oxford and Edinburgh, Cambridge and Glasgow at
Home, where some of the greatest living Masters in
every department, such as my own world-famous Professor, the now venerable Lord Kelvin, listened to my
testimony as to the power of the Gospel to make new
Creatures of the South Sea Cannibals and build them
up into the likeness of Jesus Christ. I trespassed not
into *their* spheres, where I would have been a child
and an ignoramus compared with them ; and they, on
the other hand, treated *me* with profound respect, and
even occasionally with demonstrative appreciation, in
that sphere of the moral and spiritual, the work of the
Christ-Spirit and its influence on the lowest and most
degraded of human beings, wherein I had some right
to speak with authority. This was my " one " talent,
in the presence of such men ; and I "traded" with it,
that the Name of my Saviour might be honored more
and more, in the Halls of Letters, and in the Temples
of Art and Science.

By the general desire of my fellow Missionaries on
the New Hebrides, I had visited Britain ten years before, for the express purpose of raising if possible
£5,000 for a new *Dayspring*, larger than the old, and
with Steam Auxiliary Power. By the blessing of God
on my humble pleading, and very largely in direct an-

swer to prayer, for I called on no one privately for donations, there came to us in twelve months the large
sum of £10,000, of which more than one half reached
us by post. My Church in Victoria, to whom I ren-
dered an account of all, set apart £6,000 for the new
Mission Vessel, the interest to be added to capital till
such time as she might be built; while the remaining
£4,000 were devoted to the obtaining and supporting
of additional Missionaries for the New Hebrides.

But a new difficulty had emerged, and created not
only delay all these years, but no small measure of
regrettable dissension; and that was how to maintain
the Ship, and keep her floating in the service of the
Mission; for the *Dayspring*, not being allowed to
trade, had been wholly maintained by the Sabbath
Schools of the Churches having Missionaries on the
New Hebrides. The sum which they had raised annually, each Church in its allotted proportion, amounted
to £1,500, or rather more; and it was manifest that
the Steam Auxiliary would cost at least £1,000 extra
per annum. Unfriendly critics doubled that charge,
and some prophesied even treble; but level-minded
experts limited it to £1,000, and the actual facts of
experience, as to cost of maintaining the *Morning
Star* and the *Southern Cross*, in these same Pacific
Seas, tallied with their estimates.

The burning question, therefore, had been how to
raise this *extra* sum for *Dayspring* Maintenance. Our
Victorian Church proposed to increase her quota from
£500 to £750, and issued appeals to the other coöp-

erating Churches to make a similar advance. It did
not seem too much to expect, in the interests of the
Mission, all whose operations had trebled since the
original responsibility was allocated ; but they pled
inability to comply, and so the project hung fire for
ten years and more, experiments being meanwhile
made in other arrangements for the Maritime Service
of the Mission, and new interests of various kinds being thereby created, which have not tended to unity
and peace in the management of the New Hebrides.
There is peril also incurred to the highest spiritual interests of the Mission, which I daily pray God, in His
loving kindness and mercy, to be pleased to avert !

Without ascribing anything but the most ordinary
motives in the world to those who opposed the getting
of a new *Dayspring*, the situation that thus grew up is
perfectly transparent. The Australian New Hebrides
Company was employed to do the work of our Mission by their Trading Ships. In 1805—*e.g.*, we paid
to them the large sum of £2,451, 8s. 1d.; all found
money, for, without us, these Ships in their outgoing
trip to the Islands would have sailed comparatively
empty. To secure a Ship of our own would be, therefore, to deprive the Company of this handsome subsidy ; and it is but Human Nature, and implies no
necessary dishonor, that the shareholders and their
Ministerial and Missionary friends should have become
the keenest and even bitterest opponents of the new
Dayspring. Further, the headquarters of the Company being at Sydney, and the subsidy for our Mission,

as well as the money for the upkeep of our Missionaries and their families, being consequently expended
almost exclusively there, it is, from the world's point
of view, equally natural to anticipate that the very
heart and centre of the opposition has been in New
South Wales, and has concentrated itself in the Advisory Committee which sits at Sydney and is known as
The Dayspring Board.   All this, I say, was only to be
expected, if the whole transaction is to be weighed
and measured by the standards of men of the World,
instead of being put into the balances of Jesus Christ,
and estimated in the light of the spiritual and eternal
interests of the Islanders whom He has committed to
our care.

With great plausibility, this selfish opposition sought
to commend itself to a wilder circle by a Patriotic plea.
If we did not support the Trading Company, it would
fail, and the French might come on the scene and
annex the New Hebrides!   The facts of history were
forgotten or ignored, with their ominous lesson, that
other influences than trade must be brought into action
to save these Islands from France.   Did the tide of
British trade, on the Loyalty Islands, on Madagascar,
and the like, prevent their annexation by France?
Certainly not!   True, it will be a terrible calamity, not
only to our Mission but to Australasia, if France is
permitted to annex the New Hebrides; but while she
is openly preparing the way for that fatal step, Britain
and her Colonies mock at all our warnings, and treat
the whole matter with indifference, if not contempt.

New South Wales and Victoria have even withdrawn those modest subsidies from Colonial Trading Ships, whereby their Governments might have continued to manifest some little desire to save the New Hebrides from the maw of Popish France !

Even if the horror of French Annexation were to overtake us, it might be rationally contended that our Mission, instead of being implicated with the existence of a rival Trading Company, would receive more favorable consideration, if we had a Steam Auxiliary Ship devoted entirely to spiritual services, ministering to, say, twenty-four Mission Families, with their Lay Assistants and all belongings and dependents.

But, after all, such reasonings do not even touch the very heart of the matter; and men who never go deeper than these cannot understand our aims, and are in no position to criticise them, however loudly they may abuse or oppose us. It is the spiritual and eternal welfare of our poor Islanders that is at stake, in the question of *Dayspring* or no *Dayspring;* at least that is my immovable conviction, and, apart from that, no argument on the other side has or can have much consideration at my hands. With a Mission Ship of our own, for the New Hebrides, as for every other Mission in these Pacific seas, we can visit our Stations, as the interests of God's work may require ; we can visit and cheer the Native Teachers at their lonely out-posts amongst Heathen Villages ; we can deliberately visit and open up Pioneer Stations, where Heathenism still reigns, and plant there our young Missionaries and their Helpers ; we can dissociate our Ship and her crew from the drunkenness, profligacy, and profanity of the ordinary crews of Trading Vessels ; we can prevent the sale of Fire-Arms and Intoxicants, in barter with the Natives ; and, in a single word, we can make the Mission Ship, in all her ways and surroundings, an adjunct to the work of the Missionary, and a herald of the Kingdom of God among the Islanders, alike on God's Day of Rest, and on every day of the week— and all this in a manner and to a degree, that is not within human possibility if we be deprived of our own *Dayspring*, and thrown back upon ordinary Trading Ships.   This, and this alone, goes to the bottom of the whole controversy.

Consequently, the men who opposed us never seriously denied what we here affirm, or attempted to answer our arguments.   On the contrary, they practically gave away the whole case by perilling everything on the question of expense.   All we urged might be unassailably true, but the cost was prohibitory !   The money could not be raised, or, if it could, it would be positively sinful to spend so much on such a Mission !   My blood often tingled to my finger tips, to hear this urged by self-indulgent and purse-proud men, who spent every year, on the pleasures of this perishing life, more than all that was required for the *Dayspring* and the four and twenty Mission Families, and the hundred thousand New Hebrideans, to whom she was to minister as the white-winged Servant of the Gospel of Jesus.   Nor was my mood much calmer when this same thing was urged by Ministers and Office-Bearers of the Church, at Home and in the Colonies, who carry on their labors amidst the inspiring surroundings and associations of their happier lot; who criticise Missions and their management from the safe and cozy retreat of their libraries and armchairs; who by post and telegraph are in touch with those most dear to them every day, yea, every hour; and many of whom never denied themselves one of the necessities of life, nor one of their own perhaps foolish luxuries, for the sake of the Lord Jesus and His cause,—never allowed themselves to suffer, even to the extent of one poor pennyworth, even for the length of one passing day, for the love they bore to God or to their fellows. I fear that I am an impatient reasoner, when creatures of this type cross my path. Alas, they too much abound, to the shame of the Church, and for the scorn of the World!

Coming back, therefore, to Britain, with these ten years of delay to be accounted for, I did in all my Addresses frankly avow, that, in my judgment the main obstacle, if not the only one, was the lack of this extra £1,000 per annum for Maintenance. Friends on every side started up, and thrust upon me the proposal, that those who had subscribed the money to build the ship were quite willing to subscribe yearly to assist in maintaining her. I took the whole matter to my Lord in special prayer. It was borne in upon me to let the proposal be fully known, and I felt myself bound to conclude that if, in a spontaneous way, the sum of

£1,000 were provided, with any hope of permanent
interest, to renew it from year to year, *that* would be
to me at least the demonstration of the Gideon's
Fleece, that God, who had through His people presented the Ship to our Mission, was opening up a way
for her yearly Maintenance.

A Circular Letter on the *Dayspring* Maintenance
Fund was accordingly drawn up, and issued to all correspondents and supporters by my British Committee.
Certificates for Three-Penny Shares in the *Dayspring*,
to be renewed annually, were widely circulated in Sabbath Schools. And, without further organization or
appeal, the answer to our prayers was almost instan-
taneously forthcoming. My Honorary Treasurer had
the needed £1,000 already paid, and sufficient prom-
ises for the immediate future. We were empowered
to promise this for Maintenance, if the *Dayspring*
were duly placed on the scene. If not, the money
was to be returned to the donors, or by them allocated
to other departments of the Mission enterprise. If, in
all this, we had not the guidance of God, I know not
how to trace His hand!

Other Providential signs were not awanting. I called
one day, at Liverpool, on a generous Christian gentleman, to thank him personally for a sum of £50 sent
to the Mission. The thought or purpose of seeking
more money from him had never once entered my
brain! He questioned me carefully about the needs
of the Mission, the accommodation of the proposed
Ship, and all our plans. Then he closed our interview

thus: " I am convinced that you cannot buy or build a sufficient Mission Vessel for £6,000, and I wish you to add this in order to secure a larger and a better Ship." He handed me his check for £1,000! In tears of joy, I thanked God and His dear servant, but hinted something about preferring it rather for the first year's Maintenance Fund, but he repeated that this was to secure a larger and better Ship, adding: " Receive this as from God, and the other will come also."

Again, my dear friend Lord Overtoun, who had presided over two Meetings that were addressed by me, entered one morning into a Railway Car by which I was travelling, and sat down beside me. At the close of a happy and very friendly conversation, he added: "Lady Overtoun and I gave you £200 toward the building of the Mission Ship; and now, after talking the matter over, we have resolved to give you £100 per annum for five years to help to pay for her Maintenance."

My soul overflowed with praise to God, and with thanks to those whose hearts were thus in His keeping. To me, and to all my fellow Helpers, it seemed to be plainly the will of the Lord. We reverently believed that this was God's doing, and no mere plan of ours. He had given the *Dayspring* in a present to the New Hebrides; and now He had provided for her Maintenance. We were convinced at that time, and, despite all that has happened since, we are still convinced, that the Divine voice was infallibly saying, Go forward!

I returned to Victoria in the autumn of 1894. To the Assembly of the Presbyterian Church at Melbourne I gave my first public account of my Tour Round the World as their Missionary and Representative. At the close of my address, I handed to the Moderator a check for £12,527, 4s. 2d., as the fruit of the Collections and Donations at my Public Meetings —the offerings of the people of God from all these lands, to be used for completing the evangelization of the New Hebrides. To this I added a deposit of £1,000,—part of the profits of my book, but for the time locked up in our Australian Banks. As this money all came to me through those Congregations and Assemblies which I addressed as Missionary Representative of the Church in Victoria, I regarded it as belonging to my Church and as placed entirely under their control. I had no right to exercise any further authority over it, save only thus far, that it could not honorably be spent in any other way than on the New Hebrides Mission. The donors had again and again protested that they wanted to hear me on that Mission and on nothing else—that they had many other opportunities of giving to the other great Missions in India, China, and Africa, and that what they gave through me was for the New Hebrides. I handed over the money; I delivered their message; and there, so far, my responsibility ceased.

But that sum, vast as it may seem, represented only half the generosity of the Churches of Britain and America during these three fruitful years. Side by side with Public Collections and the like, another stream of liberality had been constantly flowing. The readers of my *Autobiography* responded liberally to the appeal of my British Committee, and poured donations into their hands or mine, almost entirely by post, till, from readers of my book alone, *The John G. Paton Mission Fund*, gave me on leaving a check for £12,000. These donations were placed entirely at my personal disposal, under one condition only—that I must use them for the extension of Mission work on the New Hebrides. For the management of this sum, I obtained the sanction of the General Assembly to the preparation of a legal Deed. It is held by the Finance Committee of the Victorian Church, under those conditions,—that I only can operate on it for the extension of the work of God on the New Hebrides, while I live; and that after my decease they can use it, but only for these same purposes; thus fulfilling, as faithfully as may be, the wishes of those Christian souls who sent this money to me from all corners of the world.

In addition to these two large branches of our *General Fund*, there had come to myself or to my British Committee very considerable sums for Special Funds. Notably these two:—the *Native Teachers' Fund*, designed to pay a small yearly salary, formerly of £6, but now beginning at that figure and after two years' faithful service rising to £8, to each of those Converts to whom God had given the capacity and the call to become Helpers to the Missionary in School and Church, and

in many cases Pioneers of the Cross where no white
Missionary had ever gone : and also, the *Dayspring
Maintenance Fund*, already referred to and described.
The latter of these two was, of course, retained in the
hands of the British Committee at my call, till such
time as the Churches and the Mission Synod decided
for or against a Mission Vessel. The former they continue to administer, at my direction and under my
sanction, through one of the Missionaries on the Islands, who acts as their treasurer and agent. So far
as the annual donations will allow, we freely grant to
every Missionary all the assistance in our power for
the training and maintaining of these Native Evangelists, many of whom are destined to become the future
Pastors of the people. Up till now our difficulty has
been to find enough of suitable and reliable Native
Teachers to be allocated to the Churches, Bible Classes,
Sunday Schools, and individual Christians, willing to
support them. But we hope for great things from the
TRAINING COLLEGE recently opened on Tangoa under
Dr. Annand, one of our ablest and most devoted Missionaries ; and my British Committee have undertaken
to pay the salary of his Assistant, £150 per annum,
with my cordial approval. Many prayers are uplifted
daily for this Missionary Institute on the New Hebrides, at the very heart and centre of these Cannibal
Isles, that the Lord God would own it and send forth
thence trained and consecrated Evangelists to build up
and to rule the New Hebridean Church of Christ in
the days that are to be,—no longer under European

tutelage, but under Native Pastors. We would glory to lead on to that consummation, and then to pass to other fields of labor !

It is but right for me to mention, though most readers are already aware of it, that all my Helpers and Fellow Workers at Home and in America give their time and strength freely and gladly, without thought of any reward except the joy of the service. All actual outlays incurred in the on-carrying of the various schemes are, of course, met out of what we call the *General Fund ;* but every other penny, that comes to them or to me, goes directly to the extension of the Gospel on the New Hebrides. Each donation or subscription is acknowledged in our little quarterly magazine known as *Jottings,* a copy of which is posted to all our correspondents and supporters, and which is now the bond whereby God keeps us together and sustains our interest in this work—another develop·ment, not so much of our seeking, as rather thrust upon us by the necessities of the work of the Lord, which so increased that my Helpers could in no other way overtake the correspondence, or circulate the Mission news so eagerly desired. It is thus that those who unfeignedly seek to serve are led on by the Master Himself. The Pillar of Cloud and Fire still marches before us ; but, alas, how many have lost the power to behold it !

I praise God every day of my life for all these dear supporters and correspondents, far scattered in every Land, but one in heart for the salvation of the New

Hebrides. Through their generosity, my British Committee with my joyful approval have undertaken, in addition to the support of Native Teachers and the subsidy for Maintenance of *Dayspring*, to defray the entire cost of two Missionaries and their wives, and also two Lay European Assistants. Nay, if the generosity of friends should continue, they are at the moment of my writing hopefully contemplating the support of a third Missionary, with, if possible, a Lay Assistant also. These are surely God-honoring fruits from the planting of my humble book in hearts that love the Lord, and from the zeal and devotion and extraordinary gifts of our Honorary Organizing Secretary—with whom, and with all our Helpers everywhere, we reverently say, Glory to God and not unto us !

Our loving God orders everything well. But for that Fund handed over by me to the Victorian Church, I know not what would have become of the New Hebrides Mission during the intervening years, since the crash of our Australian Banks and the consequent terrible financial depression. Thousands and tens of thousands of our people were literally ruined. Money could not be obtained, even for the ordinary and inevitable expenses of our Congregations. Ministers' stipends were, on almost every hand, temporarily reduced. The Foreign Mission Committee's income fell so terribly, that nearly everything was consumed *in meeting the claims of the Mission to the Aborigines* and to the Chinese. In 1895 the contributions to the

Dayspring Fund fell in Victoria from £500 to £200, and even that was raised with difficulty. In fact, but for our Fund, the salaries of several of the Missionaries and Native Teachers would of necessity have been cancelled, and our forces withdrawn from the field. God be praised, that calamity was averted! All our Army for Jesus have been maintained at their posts; nay, additional Pioneers have actually, despite these depressions, gone forth and pierced the Kingdom of Darkness here and there with shafts of Gospel light.

On my return to Victoria all these schemes, and particularly the new proposals as to the *Dayspring*, were fully laid before the General Assembly of the Presbyterian Church at Melbourne. Though the Ship was offered as a free gift to the Mission, and the additional £1,000 *per annum* was now provided, without laying one farthing of financial burden on them or on any of the Churches concerned, yet our Victorian Church resolved to proceed with great deliberation, and to carry, if possible, the approval of all parties concerned. They entered into correspondence with each of the seven other Churches coöperating in the New Hebrides, and with each of the Missionaries on the Islands, and agreed to instruct the building of the Ship only if all, or a clear majority, cordially approved. More than ten years ago, all had sanctioned the raising of the money for a new and larger Steam Auxiliary Ship, and that sanction had never been withdrawn. But many things had happened since then; and it was at least brotherly and

6

considerate, if not absolutely obligatory, to confer with them all ere proceeding further.

The vast majority of the Missionaries at once re-affirmed their approval of the scheme. All the Churches concerned, except one, either cordially ap-proved or left the matter to the free decision of the Australasian Churches and the Missionaries on the field, in which decision they intimated that they would heartily concur. The one exception was the Church of New South Wales, influenced, as already indicated, by its close association with the Trading Company, though doubtless from motives entirely honorable, so far as individuals were concerned. What is known as *The Dayspring Board,* with its headquarters at Sydney, was also strongly opposed, and for similar reasons, too manifest to need specification here. But I cannot re-gard the opposition of that Board as either defensible or requiring to be taken into account at all. It is simply an Advisory Committee. It neither raises any money for the Ship nor for the Mission. It is the Executive, at most, of the Mission Synod and the Churches concerned; and its proper and only function is to carry out, in a helpful and business-like way, the instructions received from the Missionaries. It is absurd, therefore, that such a Board should have any vote on the question of a *Dayspring* or no *Dayspring,* any more than would a paid Agent executing the orders of the Missionaries for articles of merchandise. A delicate sense of honor should have made them feel this, and act accordingly, instead of becoming, as they did, not only avowed opponents of the scheme, but, in some cases, even bitter partisans and unscrupulous antagonists. For myself, I frankly say that the opposition of a Board so constituted should not only be discounted, but should be wholly ignored.

The Victorian Church, therefore, through its Foreign Mission Committee, ordered the *Dayspring*. She was built by Messrs. Mackie & Thomson on the Clyde, under the instructions and the personal supervision of John Stephen, Esquire, of Linthouse. Better, more skilled, more reliable advice could not be obtained in Britain. It was all gratuitously and ungrudgingly given for the sake of the Mission, and we felt deeply indebted for the same. The new Steam Auxiliary *Dayspring*, on her completion, was exhibited to friends, subscribers, and Sabbath Scholars, at Glasgow, at Ayr, at Belfast, at Douglas, and at Liverpool. Thousands upon thousands of people flocked to see the little Missionary Ship, and to wish her God-speed. She was universally admired. The Public Press commented on her trim appearance, substantial workmanship, and perfect adaptation to the service for which she was destined. She had been built and equipped within the £7,000 set apart for her construction. She had every necessary accommodation for Officers and Crew, for Missionaries and their Families, and for Native Teachers; and when she sailed away from Liverpool, the representatives of my British Committee, upon whom had lain the heavy burden of all the details, praised God that the plans and toils of so many years had at last been

brought to so auspicious an issue. It marked the beginning of a new era, it was hoped, in the Conversion of
the New Hebrides, and the little Ship was borne away
on the wings of prayer and praise !

She performed the Ocean voyage to the highest
satisfaction of all her Officers. At Melbourne she was
welcomed with much enthusiasm. On her first trip to
the Islands, the hearts of our Natives thrilled with
great joy at the sight of their own Gospel Ship. On
her second visit, her powers and capacities were most
severely tested, and her adaptability to the needs of
the Mission. She had to call at all our Stations, and
carry up to Aneityum all the members of the Mission
for the Annual Synod in the month of May. She had
on board fifty passengers, forty adults, and ten children, exclusive of the Native Teachers and their
families, and, after the Synod, she had to carry all
these back again to their several scattered Stations.
It was the unanimous and decided opinion of all concerned, that, during no previous Synod Trip under
any service, had we ever enjoyed the same comfort
and the same happiness. There was thanksgiving, on
every hand. The dissensions of the past were buried.
The Mission Synod had now their own Ship; and
they unitedly resolved to turn her to the best possible
account in the Cause of Jesus and for the speedy
Evangelizing of the New Hebrides. Our hearts were
at rest. We turned aside to other labors, thanking
God that in all this many prayers had been answered,
many tears had borne precious fruit. The *Dayspring*

was the crown and complement of our Missionary Enterprise for the salvation of these Islands—God bless her !

Our dear little Mission Ship performed her third trip also with perfect safety, and with much satisfaction to all the Missionaries. Her new Captain, who had formerly been her first Officer, and who in his earlier days had sailed these same Seas in the *Southern Cross*, was a great favorite alike amongst the Missionaries and the Natives; thoroughly capable, firm yet gentle, deserving and commanding universal respect. The Ship had, as the result of experience, been in some matters overhauled and readjusted, to meet special requirements; and her fourth Voyage was entered upon with hope and joy. She was loaded with provisions for the Missionaries and their Families, with wood for the building of their Houses and Schools, and with whatsoever was most urgently required by them for three months to come. So that at every Station, on every Island, the eyes of our beloved Missionaries and their Converts were eagerly looking out across the Seas for the flag of the dear little *Dayspring*.

Alas, they looked in vain ! She struck on an uncharted reef, not far from New Caledonia,—a disaster against which no skill and no experience could guard, in those not yet thoroughly explored and ever-changeful Seas. Her Officers and Crew did everything that men could do to save her, and struggled on till all hope had perished. With sore hearts, they at last provisioned and manned the two boats, and committed

themselves to the deep—agreeing on certain general
lines of action, that, please God, they might again
come together and be rescued.   In a very short time,
after they had withdrawn, a high wind and a heavy
sea working together completed her destruction, and
they beheld the dear little *Dayspring* plunging head-
foremost from the reef into the Sea, and disappearing,
masts and all, within the hungry Ocean.

The Captain's boat ran to an island for safety, and
was, ere long, picked up, and he and all his men safely
returned to Australia.   The other boat had a dreadful
voyage.   More than once she was overturned, and left
them all struggling in the Sea.   For fourteen days
and nights, without almost any food, without any possibility of rest, bareheaded in a broiling sun, the poor
fellows endured suffering and untold distress; till, at
length, by a well-nigh miraculous Providence, they ran
ashore on the coast of Queensland, and were saved.
Blessed be God, though our dear little *Dayspring*, with
all her belongings, her Library, her Mission Harmo-
nium, Lord Kelvin's magnificent Compass, and the
books, the furnishings, and the food of our beloved
Missionaries, lay sleeping in the Ocean's bed—no
father's or mother's heart was wrung with the memory
of some precious Son buried with her there.   We
were all spared that agony, and we continue to praise
God that the wreck of the *Dayspring* cost not a single
human life.

It does not need that I should inform the Reader of
the preceding pages that this wreck was, in all the

circumstances, one of the bitterest sorrows of my life.
I am not ashamed, considering my views of its spiritual value as the Handmaid of the Gospel in completing Christ's Mission on the New Hebrides, to confess
that I showed as much emotion, though in a different
way, when I heard the sorrowful news, as did the
Christian Natives at Lenukel, when they rolled themselves in anguish on the sands, and set up a death-
wail as if they had lost their dearest friend. It re-
quires very little imagination to realize the scene, as
the news was borne from Isle to Isle, and to hear one
long, deep, and heart-breaking cry resounding throughout the New Hebrides—" Alas for the Gospel Ship !
Alas for our dear little *Dayspring!* Alas for the
white-winged Herald of the Cross ! "

For one, though firmly believing that her loss was
a great blow to all the higher interests of our Mission,
I was able to say : "The Lord gave and the Lord
hath taken away:"—but yet, God forgive me, it was
very hard to add : " Blessed be the Name of the Lord."
But never, in my deepest soul, did I for a moment
doubt that in His hands all must be well. Whatever
trials have befallen me in my Earthly Pilgrimage, I
have never had the trial of doubting that perhaps, after
all, Jesus had made some mistake. No! my blessed
Lord Jesus makes no mistakes! When we see all
His meaning, we shall then understand, what now we
can only trustfully believe, that all is well—best for us,
best for the cause most dear to us, best for the good
of others and the glory of God. Still, my tears would

flow when I thought of the dear little *Dayspring*, the fruit of ten years of prayers and toils, the gift of God's people throughout the world to our beloved Mission, tumbled from that reef and lying at the bottom of the Sea. And I felt comforted to think that He, who wept with the mourning Sisters at the grave of Lazarus, did not rebuke their tears, but soothed them by weeping with them—" Jesus wept."

Wisely or otherwise, all parties seemed to embrace at once the conclusion that this Shipwreck should furnish the occasion for reconsidering the whole question of a Mission Vessel or no Mission Vessel for the New Hebrides. For the time, arrangements had again to be resumed for the services of the Trading Company ; and the interval was to be utilized in consulting the Mission Synod on the Islands, and the Churches concerned, in the light of the experience gained, whether another *Dayspring* should be built or not. I must openly affirm that this policy never commended itself to my judgment, nor even yet can I see its wisdom. With the Insurance, though limited to the inadequate sum of £2,000 much against my will by the Committee at Melbourne, and with the other Funds for the *Dayspring* still on hand, besides the Free-Will Offerings that poured in on us from friends everywhere, we could have ordered and paid for a New Ship without one hour's delay. We had the assent of the Churches and the approval of the Missionaries, and should have gone forward, as if the wreck had never happened. God seemed Himself to be clearly pointing the way. Within a few hours, after the disaster was cabled to Britain, a lady in London sent a check for £1,000 to my Home Committee, "to build or buy a new and larger ship!" Other generous offers were also pressed upon us; and the money is at this moment lying in the Bank awaiting a decision. We could then, and can now, present to the Mission another *Dayspring*, as a free gift from those throughout the world to whom God has endeared the Mission on the New Hebrides.

But I was powerless to resist the policy of delay, the consequences of which I cannot but fear, whatever the ultimate decision may be, as highly disastrous to our Mission. Should the vote be in favor of another Ship, the delay will have so damped the interest of supporters, that my British Committee may find it extremely difficult to revive subscriptions and secure the promised £1,000 *per annum* towards the Maintenance Fund. Should the vote be unfavorable, the dissension amongst the Missionaries and the Churches, and the seesaw policy in the Management of the Mission, will so shake the confidence of the Christian Public, that all our funds are bound to suffer, and the welfare of the Mission be seriously crippled. I do, therefore, most earnestly pray and hope that there may be unity, at whatever cost to my personal predilections; for the spectacle of a disloyal Minority, undermining and destroying the work of the Majority, is enough to bring on our cause the contempt of men, if not also the curse of God. And at the same time, I cannot but fervently desire that the mind of the Synod on the Islands and of the Churches in the Colonies, at Home, and in Nova Scotia, may be clear and decided in favor of a Mission Ship, for the highest welfare of the Church of God on the New Hebrides.*

Experience has demonstrated that a perfectly suitable Vessel can be constructed for, say £8,000, that is, fifty tons larger than the Ship we have lost. Experience has further demonstrated that she can be maintained for £2,500 per annum, or even less. Our opponents must therefore lay aside their speculative figures, and cease to say that her building may cost £10,000, and her yearly maintenance not less than £5,000. The *Dayspring* lived long enough to slay these two wild fabrications. Now then, let them be buried with her in the Sea! It is purely and simply a question of whether, in the interests of the Kingdom of God on the New Hebrides, and in order to cut off our work there from all degrading association with Sabbath-breaking and grog-selling Trading Ships, we should or should not accept the free-will offerings of the People at Home to build for us, and to help us to maintain, a Mission Ship of our own. I never can believe it possible to imagine any other answer but one —if that issue were clearly contemplated, and judgment pronounced, *apart* from all other considerations, whether personal, self-interested, or merely worldly.

Thus far, as part of my Life-Story, and that every

* The Synod on the Islands (May, 1897) have voted *for* a New Mission Ship by a majority of 13 against 2.—EDITOR.

reader may comprehend my aims, it seemed necessary to explain, to argue, and even to criticise. But all further reference here is needless. Ere this page is published, the final decision will probably have been announced. I can truly say that my Lord knows how sincerely I desire a clear and final decision, whether for or against another * *Dayspring;* and that, such having been given, I pledged myself beforehand to accept it as His will, and, under it, to do all that in me lies to promote during my remaining days, the true welfare of the Mission of Christ to the New Hebrides. *Dayspring*, or no *Dayspring*, these souls must be won for Jesus!

And now, since this in all human probability is the closing Chapter of my humble Life, so far as it shall ever be written by me, therefore ere I lay down my pen, let me dwell with unalloyed delight on a few pictures of facts that rise before me, illustrative of the work of God at large throughout the New Hebrides. In all my journeyings, and in all my talks and writings, though of necessity personal experiences bulked somewhat largely, yet every candid hearer or reader will bear witness that I was eager and careful to pay unstinted honor to all my fellow laborers on these Islands; many of whom, men and women too, I truly regard before God as amongst the noblest Servants of the Lord Jesus that I have ever known, or expect to know,

---

* The General Assembly at Melbourne (November, 1897) resolved by a majority of one to delay for twelve months before deciding either for or against a new *Dayspring*.—EDITOR.

on this Earth. God be with them, one and all; and though, on questions of policy and management, some of them may differ from me, I would gladly spend my last ounce of strength in promoting the spiritual interests of their work at every Station, and contributing to their personal happiness and prosperity, if it be in my power in any way to do so. All this, on both sides, we thoroughly know and understand, as becometh the Ambassadors of Christ to the Heathen World. I am never happier than when, as now, I try to picture the work of God on all the Isles of the New Hebrides, and show our friends and supporters in every Land some of the fruits of their money and their prayers.   .

At North Santo, we see Mr. Noble Mackenzie and his wife with hope and faith unfurling the Banner of the Cross; and Dr. and Mrs. Sandilands at Port Philip, Big Bay, on the same great Island, by healing and by teaching, pioneering for Jesus. Mr. Bowie and his wife, from the Free Church of Scotland, are taking possession of South Santo in the name of Christ; and if the Mission Synod agrees to plant his brother, Dr. Bowie, along with his wife, sent out this year by my British Committee, on East Santo, as seems desired—this, the largest and most northerly island of the Group, with its many languages and its unknown thousands of inhabitants, will at last be ringed round with fire,—the fire of love to Jesus and to the souls of the Heathen.

Another great Island, with several languages, has in recent years been surrounded by the soldiers of the

Cross, and claimed for Christ—Mr. Watt Leggatt and his devoted wife at Aulua, Mr. Frederick J. Paton at Pangkumu, and Mr. Boyd at South West Bay—uniting their threefold forces to bring vast and populous Malekula to the feet of Jesus. Already most hopeful beginnings have been made. Christian Churches, with a few Converts, have been planted at these three Stations—the nucleus, we trust, of living branches on Earth of the Living Body of our Living Lord in the Heavenly World.

Tanna, also, has been afresh assaulted, in the name of God. Mr. Gillies and his wife are on their way to assist and to succeed Mr. Watt at Kwamera and Port Resolution; Mr. Thomson Macmillan has entered upon the field at Wiasisi, from which Mr. Gray had to retire; and Mr. Frank H. L. Paton and his devoted wife, along with their Lay Assistant, Mr. Hume, have opened a Pioneering Mission at Lenukel, on the Western coast, entirely supported by the funds of my British Committee. And our hopes beat high that Tanna, often described as the hardest Mission field in the Heathen World, is on the eve of surrendering to the Gospel of Jesus, which the fierce Tannese have so long and so savagely resisted.

To join the noble band of younger Missionaries, Dr. Agnew has also gone to the New Hebrides, an experienced and gifted and most attractive Missionary at Home, and destined, we believe, to be a fruitful worker for Jesus in the Foreign field. The preliminary expenses connected with several of these, such as

Medical and other outfit, passage money to Australia, and the like, have been gladly borne by my British Committee, thereby relieving the Churches of all initial outlays, and encouraging them to undertake their permanent support. We press forward still, never thinking we can lawfully rest till every Tribe on the New Hebrides shall have heard, each in their own language, in their Mother Tongue, the old and ever new and deathless story of Redeeming Love.

These, however, are but beginnings. Our older Stations showed, in 1895, a record of work done and sufferings borne for Jesus that might well make all Christians thrill with praise. Take a few examples only.

During the year, Mr. Michelsen of Tongoa, one of the most successful Missionaries in the field, baptized and admitted to the Lord's Table 200 Converts; while 200 more under his tuition and that of Mrs. Michelsen were being prepared for the same holy privileges. God has given them in all nearly 2,000 Converts from amongst these Cannibals, who are being built up into the faith and service of Jesus Christ. Alas, since the Queensland Government, in defiance of the solemn Protest of the Chiefs, opened this Island to the Labor-recruiting Ships, hundreds of their best and most hopeful Native Helpers have been seduced as *Kanakas* to the Sugar Plantations—and the Missionary and the Islanders alike regard them as virtually dead; so very few will ever return! Mr. Michelsen has thirty Native Teachers or Evangelists, with 1,850 pupils at-

tending the Mission Schools. During the same year,
the Converts collected from amongst themselves £25,
and handed it over for the promotion of the Gospel of
Christ; so that the labors of this devoted servant of
God, for sixteen years, are being crowned with many
tokens of blessing.

It is believed amongst us that few Missions in the
World show more interesting fruits of Evangelistic enterprise than Nguna and its Islets, under the fostering
pastorate of Mr. Milne and his most devoted and gifted
wife. There are 750 Communicants on the Church's
Roll, 1,700 regularly attending the Worship of God,
and at least 2,000 in all who have turned from Heathenism and adopted the habits of Christian Civilization.
There are thirty Native Teachers, for whose support
the Native Church raised £155, 8s. 11d. in 1895, besides giving Arrowroot for Mission purposes valued
at £120. They had thirty-seven Christian Marriages
during the year, and 100 Candidates for Membership
in the Communicants' Class. Nay, most marvellous
of all, the Church of Nguna has thirty-eight of its mar-
ried couples who have gone forth as Native Teachers
and Mission Helpers to other Islands—a Missionary
Church called out of Heathenism, thus joyfully and in-
tinctively sending forth from its own bosom Missionaries into the Heathenism beyond. Surely I am war-
anted in saying, to the praise of Jesus and of His
servants, that this is a glorious record for five and
twenty years!

On Epi, Mr. Fraser, having labored fourteen years,

had 137 Members on his Communion Roll, and 128 Candidates in his Communicants' Class; 27 Native Teachers, with 1,000 at the Day Schools, and 1,250 at the Sabbath Schools ; and his people collected amongst themselves £34 for Mission purposes. Since then, and every day, the tide of prosperity is rising on the side of Christianity, and all these figures are steadily increasing. Mr. Smail is on the other side of the same Island, and has, as the result of six years' devotion to his work, 36 Communicants in his Church, 13 Candidates for Membership, 14 Native Teachers, and 500 daily attending their Schools. They gave £7 for the work of the Mission.

Erromanga, where five Missionaries were murdered, and two of them devoured by the Cannibals, is now a Christian Island. There are 300 Communicants, 12 Elders, 40 Native Teachers, and 1,750 attending the Schools—practically the whole population. Mr. Robertson and his devoted wife have been honored of God, in completing this grand work, during the last four and twenty years.

And so on all round the Group, Island after Island being brought by patient, devoted, and rational expenditure of time, and affection, and all Gospel influences, to the knowledge of the Christian life, and thereby to Civilization. There are still four or five great Centres of Heathenism untouched. When God sends us Missionaries for these, it will then only be a question of time coupled with pains and prayer, till all the New Hebrides in all their Babel tongues, shall be heard sing-

EPETENETO,

The first native pastor in the New Hebrides

A HEATHEN CHIEF OF FUTUNA.

Showing the hair divided in many locks, tortoise-shell earrings, bead and shell necklace.

ing the praises of Redeeming Love. May my blessed Saviour spare me to see the full Dawn, if not the perfect Noon, of that happy Day!

It is easy to raise the shallow cry that the New Hebrides Mission is overmanned, as compared with India, China and Africa, as some, and very specially the same men who most keenly oppose the *Dayspring*, are persistently doing. We might answer by retort,—Your own Towns and Villages are overmanned; why not resign your charges, and go to the millions of Heathendom? But we leave that retort to others, and reply: There are differences in all these fields of enterprise, which demand specific adaptation of means to ends, and we fearlessly declare, in the face of all Christendom, that God Himself has approved of our system by the almost unparalleled results. We plant down our European Missionary with his staff at a given Station. We surround him with Native Teachers, who pioneer amongst all the Villages within reach. His life-work is to win that Island, or that People, for God and Civilization. He masters their Language, and reduces it to writing. He translates and prints portions of the Bible. He opens Schools, and begins teaching the whole population. He opens a Communicants' Class, and trains his most hopeful Converts for full membership in the Church. And there he holds the fort, and toils, and prays, till the Gospel of Jesus has not only been preached to every creature whom he can reach, but also reduced to practice in the new habits and the new religious and social

7

life of the Community. In this way has Aneityum
been won for Christ, and thoroughly Christianized;
and Aniwa, and Erromanga, and Efatè, and Nguna, and
Tongoa, and several adjoining Isles. And, humanly
speaking, there is no other way in which these Tribes
and Peoples can be evangelized. The next stage will
be that of the Native Pastorate, with a very few super-
intending European Missionaries—a stage on which,
for instance, my own Aniwa has long since practically
entered, the Elders carrying on all the work of the
Church, with an occasional visit from a neighboring
Missionary. But the foundations of Civilization and
of Christianity must either be laid and solidly built up
by a Missionary for each of these Peoples, or they will
never be laid at all.

Let our Churches then go forward on the lines which
God the Lord hath blessed. Complete the pioneering
work on the New Hebrides, bring the Gospel within
reach of every creature there, and then set free your
money and your men to do the same elsewhere. But
even in India and in China and in Africa, with their
countless millions, learn a lesson from the work on the
New Hebrides. Plant down your forces in the heart
of one Tribe or Race, where the same Language is
spoken. Work solidly from that centre, building up
with patient teaching and lifelong care a Church that
will endure. Rest not till every People and Language
and Nation has such a Christ-centre throbbing in its
midst, with the pulses of the New Life at full play.
Rush not from Land to Land, from People to People,

in a breathless and fruitless Mission. Kindle not your lights so far apart, amid the millions and the wastes of Heathendom, that every lamp may be extinguished without any of the others knowing, and so leave the blackness of their Night blacker than ever. The consecrated Common-sense that builds for Eternity will receive the fullest approval of God in Time.

Oh that I had my life to begin again! I would consecrate it anew to Jesus in seeking the conversion of the remaining Cannibals on the New Hebrides. But since that may not be, may He help me to use every moment and every power still left to me to carry forward to the uttermost that beloved work. Doubtless these poor degraded Savages are a part of the Redeemer's inheritance, given to Him in the Father's Eternal Covenant, and thousands of them are destined through us to sing His praise in the glory and the joy of the Heavenly World! And should the record of my poor and broken life lead any one to consecrate himself to Mission work at Home or Abroad that he may win souls for Jesus, or should it even deepen the Missionary spirit in those who already know and serve the Redeemer of us all—for this also, and for all through which He has led me by His loving and gracious guidance, I shall, unto the endless ages of Eternity, bless and adore my beloved Master and Saviour and Lord, to whom be glory forever and ever.

Selections from

Fleming H. Revell Company's

Missionary Lists

New York: 158 Fifth Avenue
Chicago: 63 Washington Street
Toronto: 154 Yonge Street

The Personal Life of David Livingstone.

Chiefly from his unpublished journals and correspondence in the possession of his family. By W. GARDEN BLAIKIE, D.D., LL.D. With Portrait and Map. *New, cheap edition.* 508 pages, 8vo, cloth, $1.50.

"There is throughout the narrative that glow of interest which is realized while events are comparatively recent, with that also which is still fresh and tender."—*The Standard.*

David Livingstone.

His Labors and His Legacy. By A. MONTEFIORE, F.R.G.S. Missionary Biography Series. Illustrated. 160 pages, 12mo, cloth, 75c.

David Livingstone.

By Mrs. J. H. WORCESTER, Jr., Missionary Annals Series. 12mo, paper, net, 15c.; flexible cloth, net, 30c.

Reality vs. Romance in South Central Africa.

Being an Account of a Journey across the African Continent, from Benguella on the West Coast to the mouth of the Zambesi. By JAMES JOHNSTON, M.D. With 51 full-page photogravure reproductions of photographs by the author, and a map. Royal 8vo, cloth, boxed, $4.00.

The Story of Uganda

And of the Victoria Nyanza Mission. By S. G. STOCK. Illustrated. 12mo, cloth, $1.25.

"To be commended as a good, brief, general survey of the Protestant missionary work in Uganda."—*The Literary World.*

Robert Moffat,

The Missionary Hero of Kuruman. By DAVID J. DEANE. Missionary Biography Series. Illustrated. *25th thousand.* 12mo, cloth, 75c.

Robert Moffat.

By M. L. WILDER. Missionary Annals Series. 12mo, paper, net, 15c.; flexible cloth, net, 30c.

The Congo for Christ.

The Story of the Congo Mission. By Rev. JOHN B. MYERS. Missionary Biography Series. Illustrated. *Tenth thousand.* 12mo, cloth, 75c.

On the Congo.

Edited from Notes and Conversations of Missionaries, by Mrs. H. GRATTAN GUINNESS. 12mo, paper, 50c.

Samuel Crowther, the Slave Boy

Who became Bishop of the Niger. By JESSE PAGE. Missionary Biography Series. Illustrated. *Eighteenth thousand.* 12mo, cloth, 75c.

"We cannot conceive of anything better calculated to inspire in the hearts of young people an enthusiasm for the cause."—*The Christian.*

Thomas Birch Freeman.

Missionary Pioneer to Ashanti, Dahomey and Egba. By JOHN MILUM, F.R.G.S. Missionary Biography Series. Illustrated. 12mo, cloth, 75c.

"Well written and well worth reading."—*The Faithful Witness.*

Seven Years in Sierra Leone.

The Story of the Missionary Work of Wm. A. B. Johnson. By Rev. ARTHUR T. PIERSON, D.D. 16mo, cloth, $1.00.

Johnson was a missionary of the Church Missionary Society in Regent's Town, Sierra Leone, Africa, from 1816 to 1823.

Among the Matabele.

By Rev. D. CARNEGIE, for ten years resident at Hope Fountain, twelve miles from Bulawayo. With portraits, maps and other illustrations. *Second edition.* 12mo, cloth, 60c.

Peril and Adventure in Central Africa.

Illustrated Letter to the Youngsters at Home. By BISHOP HAMMINGTON. Illustrated. 12mo, cloth, 50c.

Madagascar of To-Day.

A Sketch of the Island. With Chapters on its History and Prospects. By Rev. W. E. COUSINS, Missionary of the London Missionary Society since 1862. Map and Illustrations. 12mo, cloth, $1.00.

Madagascar.

Its Missionaries and Martyrs. By Rev. W. J. TOWNSEND, D.D. Missionary Biography Series. Illustrated. *Tenth thousand.* 12mo, cloth, 75c.

Madagascar.

By BELLE McPHERSON CAMPBELL. Missionary Annals Series. 12mo, paper, net, 15c.; flexible cloth, net, 30c.

Madagascar.

Country, People, Missions. By Rev. JAMES SIBREE, F.R.G.S. Outline Missionary Series. 16mo, paper, 20c.

Chinese Characteristics.

By Rev. ARTHUR H. SMITH, D.D., for 25 years a Missionary in China. With 16 full-page original Illustrations, and index. *Sixth thousand. Popular edition.* 8vo, cloth, $1.25.
"The best book on the Chinese people."—*The Examiner.*

A Cycle of Cathay;

Or, China, South and North. With personal reminiscences. By W. A. P. MARTIN, D.D., LL.D., President Emeritus of the Imperial Tungwen College, Peking. With 70 Illustrations from photographs and native drawings, a Map and an index. *Second edition.* 8vo, cloth decorated, $2.00.
"No student of Eastern affairs can afford to neglect this work, which will take its place with Dr. William's 'Middle Kingdom,' as an authoritative work on China."—*The Outlook.*

Glances at China.

By Rev. GILBERT REID, M.A., Founder of the Mission to the Higher Classes. Illustrated. 12mo, cloth, 80c.

Pictures of Southern China.

By Rev. JAMES MACGOWAN. With 80 Illustrations. 8vo, cloth, $4.20.

A Winter in North China.

By Rev. T. M. MORRIS. With an Introduction by Rev. RICHARD GLOVER, D.D., and a Map. 12mo, cloth, $1.50.

John Livingston Nevius,

For Forty Years a Missionary in Shantung. By his wife, HELEN S. C. NEVIUS. With an Introduction by the Rev. W. A. P. MARTIN, D.D. Illustrated. 8vo, cloth, $2.00.

The Sister Martyrs of Ku Cheng.

Letters and a Memoir of ELEANOR and ELIZABETH SAUNDERS, Massacred August 1st, 1895. Illustrated. 12mo, cloth, $1.50.

China.

By Rev. J. T. GRACEY, D.D. *Seventh edition*, revised. 16mo, paper, 15c.

Protestant Missions in China.

By D. WILLARD LYON, a Secretary of the Student Volunteer Movement. 16mo, paper, 15c.

MISSIONS, CHINA AND FORMOSA.

James Gilmour, of Mongolia.

His Diaries, Letters and Reports. Edited and arranged by RICHARD LOVETT, M.A. With three photogravure Portraits and Illustrations. 8vo, cloth, gilt top, $1.75.

"It is a vivid picture of twenty years of devoted and heroic service in a field as hard as often falls to the lot of a worker in foreign lands."—*The Congregationalist*

Among the Mongols.

By Rev. JAMES GILMOUR. Illustrated. 12mo, cloth, $1.25.

James Gilmour and His Boys.

Being Letters to his Sons in England. With facsimiles of Letters, a Map and other Illustrations. 12mo, cloth, $1.25.

Griffith John,

Founder of the Hankow Mission, Central China. By WILLIAM ROBSON. Missionary Biography Series. Illustrated. 12mo, cloth, 75c.

John Kenneth Mackenzie,

Medical Missionary to China. With the Story of the first Chinese Hospital. By Mrs. MARY I. BRYSON. With portrait. 12mo, cloth, $1.50.

The Story of the China Inland Mission.

By M. GERALDINE GUINNESS. Introduction by J. HUDSON TAYLOR, F.R.G.S. Illustrated, 2 volumes, 8vo, cloth, each, $1.50.

From Far Formosa:

The Island, its People and Missions. By Rev. G. L. MACKAY, D.D., 23 years a missionary on the island. Well indexed. With many Illustrations from photographs by the author, and several Maps. *Fifth thousand. Popular edition.* 8vo, cloth, $1.25.

China and Formosa.

The Story of the Mission of the Presbyterian Church of England. By Rev. JAMES JOHNSON, editor of "Missionary Conference Report, 1888." With 4 Maps and many illustrations, prepared for this work. 8vo, cloth, $1.75.

In the Tiger Jungle.

And Other Stories of Missionary Work among the Telugus. By Rev. JACOB CHAMBERLAIN, M.D., D.D., for 37 years a Missionary in India. Illustrated. 12mo, cloth, $1.00.

"If this is the kind of missionary who mans the foreign stations, they will never fail for lack of enterprise. . . . The book is withal a vivid and serious portrayal of the mission work, and as such leaves a deep impression on the reader."—*The Independent.*

The Child of the Ganges.

A Tale of the Judson Mission. By Prof. R. N. BARRETT, D.D. Illustrated. 12mo, cloth, $1.25.

Adoniram Judson.

By JULIA H. JOHNSTON. Missionary Annals Series. 12mo, paper, net, 15c.; flexible cloth, net, 30c.

Once Hindu, now Christian.

The Early Life of Baba Padmanji. An Autobiography, translated. Edited by J. MURRAY MITCHELL, M.A. 16mo, cloth, 75c.

William Carey.

The Shoemaker who became "the Father and Founder of Foreign Missions." By Rev. JOHN B. MYERS. Missionary Biography Series. Illustrated. *Twenty-second thousand.* 12mo, cloth, 75c.

William Carey.

By MARY E. FARWELL. Missionary Annals Series. 12mo, paper, net, 15c.; flexible cloth, net, 30c.

Alexander Duff.

By ELIZABETH B. VERMILYE. Missionary Annals Series. 12mo, paper, net, 15c.; flexible cloth, net, 30c.

Reginald Heber,

Bishop of Calcutta, Scholar and Evangelist. By ARTHUR MONTEFIORE. Missionary Biography Series. Illustrated. 12mo, cloth, 75c.

Heavenly Pearls Set in a Life.

A Record of Experiences and Labors in America, India, and Australia. By Mrs. LUCY D. OSBORN. Illustrated. 12mo, cloth, $1.50.

Persian Life and Customs.

With Incidents of Residence and Travel in the Land of the Lion and the Sun. By Rev. S. G. WILSON, M.A., for 15 years a missionary in Persia. With Map, and other Illustrations, and Index. *Second edition, reduced in price.* 8vo, cloth, $1.25.

Justin Perkins,

Pioneer Missionary to Persia. By his son, Rev. H. M. PERKINS. Missionary Annals Series. 12mo, paper, net, 15c.; flexible cloth, net, 30c.

Women and the Gospel in Persia.

By Rev. THOMAS LAURIE, D.D. Missionary Annals Series. 12mo, paper, net, 15c.; flexible cloth, net, 30c.

Henry Martyn, Saint and Scholar.

First Modern Missionary to the Mohammedans. 1781-1812. By GEORGE SMITH, author of "Life of William Carey," "The Conversion of India," etc. With Portrait, Map, and Illustrations. Large 8vo, cloth, gilt top, $3.00.

"This excellent biography, so accurately written, so full of interest and contagious enthusiasm, so well arranged, illustrated, and indexed, is worthy of the subject."—*The Critic.*

Henry Martyn.

His Life and Labors: Cambridge—India—Persia. By JESSE PAGE. Missionary Biography Series. Illustrated. *Eleventh thousand.* 12mo, cloth, 75c.

Henry Martyn.

Missionary to India and Persia. 1781-1812. Abridged from the Memoir by Mrs. SARAH J. RHEA. Missionary Annals Series. 12mo, paper, net, 15c.; flexible cloth, net, 30c.

The Conversion of India.

From Pantænus to the Present Time, A. D. 193-1893. By GEORGE SMITH, C.I.E., author of "Henry Martyn." Illustrated. 12mo, cloth, $1.50.

The Cross in the Land of the Trident.

By Rev. HARLAN P. BEACH, Educational Secretary of the Student Volunteer Movement. *5th thousand.* 12mo, paper, net, 25c.; cloth, 50c.

MISSIONS, JAPAN.

Rambles in Japan,

The Land of the Rising Sun. By Rev. Canon H. B. TRISTRAM, D.D., F.R.S. With forty-six illustrations by EDWARD WHYMPER, a Map, and an index. 8vo, cloth, $2.00.

"A delightful book by a competent author, who, as a naturalist, writes well of the country, while as a Christian and a humanitarian he writes with sympathy of the new institutions of new Japan." —*The Independent.*

The Gist of Japan :

The Islands, their People, and Missions. By Rev. R. B. PEERY, A.M., Ph.D., of the Lutheran Mission, Saga. Illustrated. 12mo, cloth decorated, $1.25.

This book does not pretend to be an exhaustive treatise of an exhaustless topic; it does pretend to cover the subject; and whosoever is eager to know the "gist" of those matters Japanese in which Westerners are most interested—the land, the people, the coming of Christianity, the difficulties and prospects of her missions, the condition of the native Church—will find it set down in Dr. Peery's book in a very interesting, reliable, instructive, and condensed form.

The Ainu of Japan.

The Religion, Superstitions, and General History of the Hairy Aborigines of Japan. By Rev. JOHN BATCHELOR. With 80 Illustrations. 12mo, cloth, $1.50.

"Mr. Batchelor's book, besides its eighty trustworthy illustrations, its careful editing, and its excellent index, is replete with information of all sorts about the Ainu men, women, and children. Almost every phase of their physical and metaphysical life has been studied, and carefully noted."—*The Nation.*

The Diary of a Japanese Convert.

By KANZO UCHIMURA. 12mo, cloth, $1.00.

"This book is far more than the name indicates. It is the only book of its kind published in the English language, if not in any language. It is something new under the sun, and is as original as it is new. It has the earmarks of a strong and striking individuality, is clear in diction, forceful in style, and fearless in criticism."—*The Interior.*

A Maker of the New Japan.

Joseph Hardy Neesima, the Founder of Doshisha University. By Rev. J. D. DAVIS, D.D., Professor in Doshisha. Illustrated. *Second edition.* 12mo, cloth, $1.00.

"The life is admirably and spiritedly written, and its hero stands forth as one of the most romantic and inspiring figures of modern times, a benefactor to his own country and an object of tender regard on our part; for it was to the United States that Mr. Neesima turned for light and help in his educational plans." —*The Examiner.*

MISSIONS, PACIFIC ISLANDS.

John G. Paton,

Missionary to the New Hebrides. An Autobiography, edited by his brother. With an Introductory Note by Rev. A. T. Pierson D.D. Illustrated. *Tenth thousand.* 2 vols., 12mo, cloth, gilt top, boxed, net, $2.00 ; *cheaper edition*, 1 vol., 12mo, cloth, $1.50.

"We commend to all who would advance the cause of Foreign Missions this remarkable autobiography. It stands with such books as those Dr. Livingstone gave the world, and shows to men that the heroes of the cross are not merely to be sought in past ages." —*The Christian Intelligencer.*

Bishop Patterson,

The Martyr of Melanesia. By JESSIE PAGE. Missionary Biography Series. Illustrated. *Thirteenth thousand.* 12mo, cloth, 75c.

James Calvert;

Or, From Dark to Dawn in Fiji. By R. VERNON. Missionary Biography Series. Illustrated. *Tenth thousand.* 12mo, cloth, 75c.

From Darkness to Light in Polynesia.

With Illustrative Clan Songs. By REV. WILLIAM WYATT GILL, LL.D. Illustrated. 12mo, cloth, $2.40.

John Williams,

The Martyr Missionary of Polynesia. By REV. JAMES J. ELLIS. Missionary Biography Series. Illustrated. *Thirteenth thousand.* 12mo, cloth, 75c.

Among the Maoris;

Or, Daybreak in New Zealand. A Record of the Labors of Marsden, Selwyn, and others. By JESSIE PAGE. Missionary Biography Series. Illustrated. 12mo, cloth, 75c.

Pioneering in New Guinea,

1877-1894. By JAMES CHALMERS. With a Map and 43 Illustrations from Original Sketches and Photographs. 8vo, cloth, $1.50.

"It reveals a splendid character, and records a noble apostolic work. It is a notable addition to our missionary literature of the high class."—*The Standard.*

James Chalmers,

Missionary and Explorer of Rarotonga and New Guinea. By WILLIAM ROBSON. Missionary Biography Series. Illustrated. *Fourteenth thousand.* 12mo, cloth, 75c.

On the Indian Trail,

And Other Stories of Missionary Work among the Cree and Saulteaux Indians. By EGERTON R. YOUNG. Illustrated by J. E. LAUGHLIN. 12mo, cloth, $1.00.

Mr. Young is well known to readers of all ages as the author of "By Canoe and Dog Train," "Three Boys in the Wild North Land," and other very popular books describing life and adventure in the great Northwest. The stories in this new book tell of some very exciting incidents in his career, and describe phases of life among the American Indians which are fast becoming things of the past.

Forty-two Years Among the Indians and Eskimos.

Pictures from the Life of the Rt. Rev. John Horden, first Bishop of Moosonee. By BEATRICE BATTY. Illustrated. 12mo, cloth, $1.00.

Vikings of To-Day;

Or, Life and Medical Work among the Fishermen of Labrador. By WILFRED T. GRENFEL, M.D., of the Deep Sea Mission. Illustrated from Original Photographs. *Second edition.* 12mo, cloth, $1.25.

"The author has been in charge of the work since its inception, and writes, accordingly, with special authority and wealth of detail, both as to the methods of work and as to the people—the fearless, patient Vikings—to whom he has dedicated his life."—*The Examiner.*

Amid Greenland Snows;

Or, The Early History of Arctic Missions. By JESSE PAGE. Missionary Biography Series. Illustrated. *Tenth thousand.* 12mo, cloth, 75c.

Kin-da-Shon's Wife.

An Alaskan Story. By Mrs. EUGENE S. WILLARD. Illustrated. *Third edition.* 8vo, cloth, $1.50.

"From beginning to end the book holds the attention. Mrs. Willard has shown herself peculiarly well qualified to write such a book."—*Public Opinion.*

David Brainerd,

The Apostle to the North American Indians. By JESSE PAGE. Missionary Biography Series. Illustrated. *Twelfth thousand.* 12mo, cloth, 75c.

South America, the Neglected Continent.

By LUCY E. GUINNESS and E. C. MILLARD. With a Map in colors and many other Illustrations. Small 4to, paper, 50c.; cloth, 75c.

Milton Keynes UK
Ingram Content Group UK Ltd.
UKHW022120161023
430741UK00005B/97

9 781015 406070